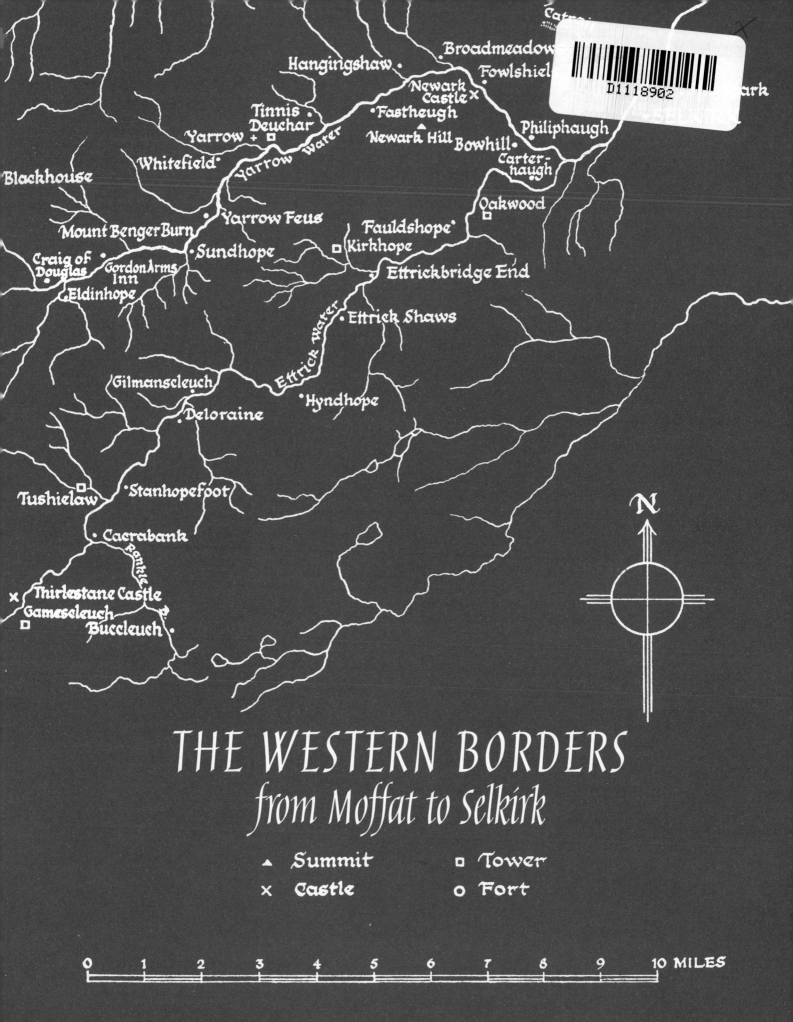

THE WESTERN BORDERS
from Moffat to Selkirk

▲ Summit   □ Tower

✕ Castle   ○ Fort

0   1   2   3   4   5   6   7   8   9   10 MILES

D1118902

MAKING FOR HOME

ALAN TAIT

Photographs by Andrea Jones

MAKING FOR HOME

A Tale of the Scottish Borders

PIMPERNEL
PRESS LTD
www.pimpernelpress.com

For Liadhain and Domnall

Pimpernel Press Limited
www.pimpernelpress.com

Making for Home copyright © Pimpernel Press Limited, 2017
Text copyright © Alan Tait, 2017

First Pimpernel Press edition 2017

Alan Tait has asserted his right to be identified as the author of this work
in accordance with the Copyright Designs and Patents Act 1988 (UK).

All rights reserved. No part of this publication may be reproduced,
stored in a retrieval system, or transmitted, in any form, or by any
means, electronic, mechanical, photocopying, recording or otherwise,
without the prior written permission of the publisher or a licence
permitting restricted photocopying. In the United Kingdom such
licences are issued by the Copyright Licensing Agency, Barnard's Inn,
86 Fetter Lane, London EC4A 1EN.

A catalogue record for this book is available
from the British Library.

Typeset in MVB Verdigris and Sweet Sans
Designed by Dalrymple

ISBN 978 1 910258 83 5
Printed and bound in China

9 8 7 6 5 4 3 2 1

Illustrations copyright © Andrea Jones, 2016 and Alan Tait
Additional photographs reproduced by kind permission:
p.8, p.67, p.73, Terence Leigh; p.22 Earl of Annandale; p.37 *Rottenrow,
Glasgow*, Audrey Walker, *c.*1955–56, silver gelatine print, Scottish
National Gallery of Modern Art Archive, presented by the artist's sister,
Mrs P.M. Black, 1987; p.39, p.122 Domnall Tait; p.59 Andrea Rose,
courtesy of the Trustees of the Little Sparta Trust;
p.80, p.84 John Reiach; p.110 Pierre Clerk

Endpapers drawn for *From the Border Hills*
by Molly Clavering, Edinburgh, 1953

HISTORICAL NOTE
7

INTRODUCTION
9

SETTING
13

HOUSE
21

OVERTURE
35

LOOKING
47

SUPPORT
63

OLD BOYS
79

PIECES
91

INSIDE
103

OUTSIDE
115

VALLEY
127

THANKS
142

HISTORICAL NOTE

Polmoodie was a farm laid out around 1762 for the 2nd Earl of Hopetoun, a notable agricultural improver, for whom John Adam built Moffat House between 1762 and 1767. Polmoodie Farm was shown on an Annandale Estate map of 1767 by the land surveyor William Tennoch who was responsible for much work on this and the adjoining Hopetoun estates.

There were three tenants who decisively formed the character taken by the farm. David Irving took up his tenancy in 1787 and in November 1791 he wrote from Polmoodie his notable letter to the Board of Agriculture. He was probably followed by Thomas Gibson around 1805 who continued until 1818 when he gave up his lease. There are copies of his letters of this time at Polmoodie. He was succeeded by Robert Johnstone before 1851, and he remained until around 1878.

In 1961, Polmoodie was sold for the first time in its history by the Annandale Estate to the Secretary of State for Scotland. It was then split between the Forestry Commission, the National Trust for Scotland and a private landowner. I bought Polmoodie, its steading and roughly five acres from the Commisssion in 1973. In 1989, I bought the forest of Polmoodie East, of 529 acres, from the Commission, and the following year acquired Birkhill and 2,978 acres. AT

For clarity's sake, I have added the following brief glossary of possibly unfamiliar words.

Blackies *Blackface sheep, a type was bred at Polmoodie in the 1780s*

Bothy *accommodation for a farm worker*

Cleuch *a small ravine*

Close *a passageway leading to a common stair*

Dyke *a wall made only of stones*

Fank *holding pen for sheep*

Greywacke *a form of very rough rock, found rather than quarried*

Hefted *where sheep have been made familiar with a certain area*

Hirsel *an area grazed by a small flock of sheep*

Hope *a small valley in the hills*

Hot-trod *tracing of stolen goods*

Lucky midden *a useful find from a refuse heap*

March *a boundary fence or wall between properties*

Reiver *robber*

Steading *farm buildings*

Stell *a shelter for sheep*

Smookey *a sneaky, hidden place*

INTRODUCTION

Keeping a diary or writing one's memoirs
when one has reached a certain age should be an obligation
imposed on us by the state.
GIUSEPPE DI LAMPEDUSA

This is a tale of three houses. One is a small tenement flat in Glasgow, the other a farm-house, and later farm, Polmoodie in the Moffat Water valley, virtually in the middle of the Scottish Borders. That of course comes to two. The third is not really a house at all but a collecting box for Dr Barnardo's homes, a thatched cottage made in papier mâché and sweetly pretty. On the roof and beside the chimney, there was a hole for coins – my savings – and this was my introduction in the 1940s to the money game, as well as to the worldly-wise precept that a house always eats money. But there was more to it than that. I think I must have liked its simple geometry and self-sufficiency and had it in mind when later faced with or possibly tempted by some large and inconvenient architectural wonder.

I should be truthful, too, for this is my second airing of such opinions: the first was in 2008 when I wrote principally about the house and especially its garden in a book called sensibly enough *A Garden in the Hills*, published by Frances Lincoln. Instead, I have now made a wider history and given greater attention to the valley, its inhabitants and their way of life in the Badlands of history. I made many mistakes in my first story and fought my battle in too limited a fashion and with too small an army. I was dismissive of my soldiers and sidelined the people with whom I worked and whom I grew to know well during the formative years of the seventies. So I have changed plan and concentrated more on both people and valley and followed a wider, literary, and more historical path that extends backwards to the Ettrick Shepherd and the Killing Times of Bloody Clavers, a favourite scoundrel in Scottish history of the seventeenth century. Nor have I neglected more recent villains such as the Forestry Commission and its stalwarts who have changed the valley from one of sheep to trees in forty years and from fourteen shepherds to one. It is a dramatic switch from the landscape of 1858, when there was barely four hundred acres of woodland – mostly scrub – scattered over the thirty eight thousand of the seven, original farms with 'their many servants and artisans'. Though not perhaps the first revolution to strike the valley, it has been certainly the most destructive.

In my earlier book, I gave an account of my near obsession with gardening and landscape, which included trees of all sorts, and an understanding of forestry large and small. I also saw the garden in that book very much as a reflection of the house and I have expanded here the complementary side of my continuing enthusiasm for houses and the

opposite: A shepherd returns from the hill at Hunterheck.

heavy baggage that came along with such an interest – the character of rooms and their contents. In this rather roundabout way, I have chosen a long way home, attempting a broader account of how things happened in the way they did and why the time span was seemingly such a long one – I suppose a good half century.

The Dr Barnardo's collecting box of the 1940s held my imagination. It was cleverly disguised – for me anyhow – as a cottage, two up, two down, thatched roof and with roses round the door. It appealed to me in a very simplistic way for I think I truly believed that it was the home of the fortunate Barnardo orphans. Its simple geometric formality stayed with me when, nearly twenty years later, I bought a Glasgow tenement flat: I seem to have acquired its frugal though hardly physical successor. The flat was only remotely pretty and, as I expected, ate rather than saved money but it was straightforward, basic and practical like any honest, collecting box. To go from one to another was to arrive in the real world where I could move on slowly, teasing myself with redundant manses and derelict farmhouses in the strangest of places to be paid for with my Barnardo coins. Matters were not made any easier or more sensible as I had, at the start, no car that I could call my own to take me to these never-never lands.

Glasgow was a city of tenements in which neighbours performed a critical role. They maintained conventions, both written and understood, and directed unobtrusively a casual form of cooperative life that offered the novice an unforgettable training in tact. Just as well, for it was needed when the next long step was boldly taken in 1973. This pushed us in at the deep end of life on a hill farm where making ends meet was hard and becoming harder for our neighbours, with the role of the outsider a difficult one where my tenement training was put to work at once. At that stage too, looking to move on in a literary way, I had just read Forster's *Howard's End* and its story of the passage from rural to suburban and of the house's guardian spirit – Miss Avery. So when we did move, I was keen to find such a guardian who could suggest and advise what was good for the house and would stand up for us in what remained of the community.

By 1975 the farmhouse at Polmoodie was in sufficient order for us to be able to stay for the odd, cold night. This was a positive milestone that I had sometimes despaired of passing or even finding. The building was a neat long rectangular box, bigger than a cottage but smaller than any manse that we had seen or been shown. We did not have many possessions and such modesty fitted well the original character of the house once the years of linoleum, brown woodwork, frosted glass and porches had been peeled back. In this way, the ripe fruit of my early years in small salerooms and minor auctions was brought to life and given a fresh sense of place. I was encouraged – cautiously by osmosis – to fill any vacuum in the rigorous style of less is more. I had in mind the outstanding example of Jim Ede's Kettle's Yard in Cambridge where Ede had run together a group of cottages in the modest shadow of a tiny Norman church to house his collection of Modern painting and sculpture, arranged in an austere, domestic setting.

I knew Kettle's Yard well in its private days, shortly before it became a small but deeply personal museum.

I was once told that in buying a house you bought its troubles and it was as well to understand that at the outset. It was just as important as any legal consideration about rights of way, or how your water came or went, or whether the telephone actually worked and where to lay the blame when it failed. Such practical matters were not found on paper but stored in some deep bottle of the past. It was worth remembering too that the house would carry the life of its inhabitants forward long after their deaths, as a kind of ghost story. It was even more the case with the land itself, where the stone and water that formed hill and river had a collective memory recalled as a map, felt as much as seen. Ownership was little more than the old chestnut of guardianship and responsibility and just about as meaningless. It was obliquely summed up by Norman MacCaig in his poem *A Man in Assynt*, 'Who possesses this landscape? – / The man who bought it or / I who am possessed by it? / False questions, for / this landscape is / masterless'.

Dr Barnardo's box in glazed porcelain rather than papier mâché.

SETTING

Almost any landscape can be reduced to its simplest elements by description. It is easy to write in bald and possibly stark terms such as hills, high or rounded; fields, large or small; water, running or still; roads, straight or twisting; large farms, small cottages and so on. It is also easy to sharpen the language to account for more historical matters where fact gives way to interpretation and motives have to be accounted for and to some extent explained. In writing in such a way, there is always the hope that a certain elusive objectivity can be found and the too obvious traps of time avoided. To describe in plain and straightforward language the house at Polmoodie is hardly difficult, but the valley and inner valley of Moffat Water, in which it sits, need to be measured by a wider perspective of words and landscape. This I have tried to do.

The valley of Moffat Water is roughly ten miles long from end to end. It starts with the small Border town of Moffat – little more than a large village – and makes a continuous rise eastwards to over a thousand feet where the hills gather together at Birkhill. The valley is U-shaped and steep-sided, gouged out by the retreating glacier grinding west in the remote past, with the last three miles forming a sub-valley that has been historically called Polmoodie. The present road, the A708, runs along the bottom of the valley and follows slavishly the serpentine course of river, the Moffat Water, itself created by the ice erosion. This road is given a historic feeling by the three humpbacked bridges of the nineteenth century, a fourth – across the Polmoodie Burn – was destroyed in the early sixties in the interests of a speedy journey elsewhere. It had been formed to connect the seven original farms and one small country house to the outside world and was roughly shown as such on an estate map of 1767 and called, modestly and truthfully, the Birkhill Path. The Path assumed a more formal role when it was surveyed in 1792 by William Crawford and published as part of a handsome map of the county in 1806.

By the second half of the nineteenth century the world had moved on and the road gained a school and schoolhouse beside the farm buildings at Roundstonefoot. They served the children within a five-mile radius well enough and no doubt helped to keep a distinct, valley character that put – misguidedly – little weight on formal education. Two further houses appeared at about the same time, both built in a similar, vaguely picturesque style to the schoolhouse. Close by, there was until the sixties, the humble cottage of a roadman whose job it had been to look after the verges and ditches, fill the

opposite: Humpback bridge on the A708 after Capplegill.

potholes and dispose of the occasional litter. However, by the 1970s both cottage and roadman were gone, leaving only a splendid bird cherry to mark their passage. The road was always a good, historical map.

Most of the seven, original farms in the greater valley were altered and extended in the nineteenth century, usually by the addition of a service wing of sorts connected to one side or the rear as at Polmoodie. In a few cases, an ambitious attempt was made to double the size of the house by duplicating the original block, one behind the other, as happened at Roundstonefoot. The most obvious difference between the two rival centuries was in height. Those of the eighteenth were one and a half storey, those of the nineteenth rarely less than two: the neighbouring farmhouse at Sailfoot was a good example of such upward mobility. Polmoodie had started out as a long rectangle, some 45 × 22 feet, with a ceiling height of never more than seven and a half feet, often a painful physical reminder of the average height of the eighteenth century farmer. The more prosperous farms had a U-shaped office court to one side, as at Bodesbeck and Crofthead, while at Capplegill a circular threshing mill was incorporated into the steading composition. But a long horizontal block that mimicked the proportions of the house was the oldest and simplest arrangement; a sheep farm had comparatively few needs and they were easily and inexpensively met. A small byre and offices, for example, cost £62 to build in 1828, and such an expense was often set against the rent, so there was little capital outlay required from the tenant. All of the farms were traditionally painted white, as they are now – whitewashed every year, with the steading and house forming an irregular group, piloting the way up the valley. If these farms were to be arranged in some agricultural improvement stakes, then Polmoodie was pretty well at the bottom and left further behind when the early twentieth century was reached. There it stayed, sticking to convention and hoping for better days.

The greatest change for all the farms in the valley was the arrival of forestry. The original Forestry Commission had been set up in haste in 1919 to make sure there was soft timber for the next war – largely for use as pit props in the mines. It was much the same response as the need for hardwood – for ships – after the Napoleonic one in the nineteenth century and similarly behind the times. Its particular prey was 'wasteland', that is the hills. One farm after another fell to the blanket planting of the conifer and the brown colours of the hills gave way to the unchanging green of the Sitka spruce – much as happened over the hill in Eskdalemuir where the valley was planted as a gloomy illustration from Grimm's *Fairy Tales*. The hillside pattern of dykes and stells, built to manage the sheep, shrank or disappeared altogether under such dense and uniform plantations. The amount and quality of the remaining hill-grazing declined and the scrub woodland of the remote cleuchs retreated and vanished. Bracken increased too in response to the more casual management of the sheep and the summer task of scything when the weather was poor but the days long was abandoned – totally by the late 1960s. There are now few shepherds – perhaps one where there had been two or three on each farm – and their collies are heard as rarely as their master's exasperated language.

The animal world also altered. The historic Blackface breed of sheep slowly gave ground to the more profitable crosses of the Cheviot – better weight and wool – and along the edges of the plantations roe deer have arrived, coming from the east and pushing the wild goats to higher and even more inaccessible land with their companions in adversity, the blackcock. And along with the deer, appeared the other sportsman's prey – the pheasant – often hapless refugees from several distant and commercial shoots who adjusted slowly and so fatally to life in the wild. The fish have followed the animal migration too. Salmon and brown trout have departed the river that has become too acid for their liking from the encroaching conifer plantations, and restocking on any scale has not been successful. Little has tempted the fish back to stay – apart from the odd pool of nervous minnows.

Such an abrupt transition from high moorland to large scale forestry has had its share of casualties. Some adapted better than others, the brown hare still hangs on as do the red grouse, barn owls and the swifts in the roofs of the farm buildings. The red squirrel comes and goes and its arch enemy the grey has been sighted. On the river, little life is left despite all the banking and imaginative engineering of the local Fishery Board who remain hopeful and determined. But it has left slim pickings for the mink or the heron or even for that matter the old-fashioned poacher with his gaffe. Still, the noisy oyster-catchers have remained faithful through thick and thin and there is always a pair to be found nesting on the stones of the river bank. They have migrated from the large colony on St Mary's Loch to the east and their arrival is our most reliable sign of spring. In such a fashion, a balance has been casually struck between the old and new, life has continued though the feet and wings may be different. What has changed, and continues to change, is the natural cycle. Whereas in the past woods remained undisturbed for a century or so, now every forty or fifty years most of the timber is harvested and replanted and the destruction both tremendous and noisy. There is little choice if the Forestry Authority, a half-brother of the Commission, is to grant the mandatory felling licence and this makes sure a blight remains a blight – it has never been able to see the wood for the trees. All of which has given the whole valley a constant, unseasonal sense of change in shape, colour and sound, and the upheaval has led to an uneasy restlessness that has violated the time-less spirit of the sanctuary of the hills.

There are now no tenant farms left in the valley. The change was a fairly speedy one, faster after 1945, and within twenty years the last of the traditional landlords departed to be replaced by the Commission, eager to direct and assume a range of national rather than local responsibilities. On its heels came the charities, first the National Trust and then the Border Forest Trust. It was the horse being replaced by the tractor all over again. Farms – undermanned and undercapitalised – were left to their own devices and the whole character of the valley altered, socially as well as physically. Three ceased to be

View up the Moffat Water valley to Bodesbeck Law from Waterside.

farms: one became a fish farm, a tariff duly posted beside the road, another bred Welsh ponies. At Craigieburn, Sailfoot and Roundstonefoot, the farmhouses were sold off and the hill land planted, as indeed happened at Polmoodie, and the shepherds retired reluctantly. The only real survivor from the woody wreckage was Bodesbeck where apart from the odd shelterbelt there was no commercial forestry. Superficially, and to the casual passer by, such developments seemed perhaps for the better with the farmhouses and their gardens given a new lease of life that brought them closer to the idealised vision of the Scottish bed and breakfast brochure. The same was true of the former schoolhouse and its schoolroom and even of the Commission's brief excursion into smallholding with a tied house; all varied their names and took on more affluent-seeming roles. But such activity caught the roving eye of the local authority and overnight Roundstonefoot and its cottages were classed as a 'hamlet' in a grotesque parody of the planned village of the eighteenth century. Such a designation allowed scope for a few roadside houses. A couple of such architectural cripples duly appeared that added nothing to the planner's ham-fisted attempt at a villagey feel: and that was more or less that.

A different key to the past was the road. It had evolved from farm track to road in the late eighteenth century but remained little more than a cart's width – about six feet – for most of the following century as the humpback bridges and edgeless verges prove disconcertingly. And so it stayed until the 1920s with the odd corner straightened and the ditches cleared and improved. But it was in no state to take on the later car culture and was at the mercy of the relentless white van and the timber traffic, both fast and furious, or even the biker convoys in their spirited search for lost youth. The road was now asked to do two things that were at loggerheads with each other: to continue as the traditional tourist route for buses, caravans and the like making for the Grey Mare's Tail waterfall but also accommodate the expanding east–west, commercial traffic, often directed – mischievously I think – by the unquestioning satellite navigation installed in the lumbering trucks. The road, laid on the old track of the eighteenth century one that wandered over humpback bridges and through a farmyard, needs a new lease of life or – better still – radical rethinking, if they are not the same.

At eight miles from Moffat, the road was our lifeline to which the car was attached. There was an irregular bus service to Selkirk and the eastern Borders, and then a post bus from Moffat, and then nothing. Cars had little appeal, especially in any technical sense, and this was foolish for we relied upon them almost completely. The first one was a Citroen, called questionably an Ami, and a descendant of the formidable and hardy Deux Chevaux of which it was neither. It was temperamental and disliked damp. The engine was constructed so that the electric component was at the bottom, closest to the ground, and first into any puddle or flood, of which there were plenty at any time of the year. It was followed by a further two of the same make and type, rather handsome cars with plenty of carrying space and five doors but designed for a

Mediterranean climate. As a lifeline they were hopeless yet it took a while before reason prevailed and we went German.

For most travellers, journey's end is the car park of the Grey Mare's Tail. This provided at once an oblique view of the gushing waterfall above and an even better one – after a short and parallel walk upwards – of its source in Loch Skene. Its appeal has been a long one since it was organised in the nineteenth century with horse-drawn vans departing from the rival Moffat hotels – the Annandale and Cranston's – for an afternoon trip throughout the summer months. To whet the tourist appetite, there were plenty of prints of one sort or another that showed a hissing torrent in a romantic setting of rocks and cloud of which the best were probably those of D.O. Hill that illustrated the 1858 guide. After that date, photography and realism took over with the rather wishy-washy watercolours of *Birkhill – A Reminiscence*, of 1899, all too typical of the sort. Most guides were underpinned by accounts of the rare flora and fauna of the surrounding hills, seriously listed in *The New Statistical Account* of 1843, and again in the *Narrative of a Ramble among the Wild Flowers of the Moffat Hills* in 1857. For the bolder, perhaps more historical spirits, there was the Covenanting tradition. In the 1670s government troops under the command of the unpopular Colonel Graham of Claverhouse, the anti-hero of Hogg's alarming novel *The Brownie of Bodebeck*, had hunted successfully the radical dissidents along the hill tops and among the hidden valleys. The punishment was execution on the spot and this produced a fair crop of martyrs for their cause. So much so that the Covenanters are still remembered yearly by Blanket Sunday, a short service held in the more accessible hills with the preacher protected from sun or rain by a blanket. Still, much of the spirit of rebellion remains in the air for those earnest hill walkers who smell the toxic gust of liberty amongst the heathery summits and become, for an afternoon at least, the revolutionaries of the past. I have often thought the sheep must share the same lawless feeling from time to time.

HOUSE

There has always been confusion about what the past may mean. For some, it is little more than day dreaming, and about as unhealthy, for others an inseparable part of any future, but for me it has always been close – almost an everyday language, difficult but lively and inventive. For better or worse, I have always thought of my houses in such a way. And so it was easy for me to stand beside the rattling sheep grid at Polmoodie, and look downhill to the east where the hills close and form a valley within a valley like some Chinese box, and daydream. From there, I can see both road and river running in tandem from one end to the other as the visual tools of history, changing shape and renewing themselves as time goes by, almost a piece of land art by Richard Long. In fact, it was Long who wrote in *Touchstones* in 1983, that a 'walk marks time with an accumulation of footsteps. It defines the form of the land. Walking the roads and paths is to trace a portrait of a country'.

This valley is an empty one except for our house and a cottage hidden at either end, one east, the other west, with three miles between them. It is not a wilderness in any sense, far too many hands have been at work for too long. The retreating glacier left behind the hanging valley of the Grey Mare's Tail, followed by the bits and pieces of history in the graptolite fossils of the moraine and the flat-topped hills that form the steep sides. Into this have come animals and men who have used the hollows and stones for shelter and later formed the walls and buildings from the greywracke outcrops– the dykes, stells, fanks and cottages – in every sense the raw material of history.

Beyond the house and close to the sheep grid, there are some old terracing and lazy-beds alongside the remains of a probable cottar township – a loose collection of small cottages. Not much perhaps, but they are the tangible traces of my predecessors and their way of life. They were largely graziers – first of goats, then of sheep – on the surrounding hills during the summer. Some cultivated the better ground where they settled, perhaps prospered, but not sufficiently to survive the agricultural revolution of the eighteenth century when the modern estate was put together from their pastures and casual villages. The seven former sheep farms are largely the result of such rural depopulation. The feral goats that hang on along the hill tops are the wild ghosts of such people and their lost way of life – the road a phantom footway that led from one community to the other. Such a path probably changed little after it became a formal piece of topography, shown sketchily on an estate map of 1767 as the Birkhill Path with an arrow running improbably straight

opposite: Looking west to Moffat and the Annandale hills.

to the east. Its origins then were social and practical, unlike the more distant and imperial roads built by the Romans with other ends in mind. It lacked as well the solid stone base needed by the legions and their chariots continually on the move, and was instead the work of barely-shod Celtic feet and their rough-hoofed ponies. Then followed the small packhorses and finally carts and wagons: it was the road that continued while its travellers were forgotten – something the walking artist Hamish Fulton would have enjoyed. It followed its wet twin – the river – and both river and road were governed by the weather though in very different and never easy ways. But of the two, the river was the unfailing and loyal guide, endlessly adaptable, and companionable, murmuring to itself when the road stayed silent.

Silence has always been an accepted part of the wilderness, as has emptiness. Both come from dispossession and de-population in some form or another and live among the ruins of a now empty landscape. They are part of the history of this valley and never hard to find. At the sheep grid, beneath the nettles and dense bracken, lie the footings of a gable and the casual outlines of other shelters, all set around the fresh water of the unfailing well. These shelters formed a summer village and kept depopulation at bay for

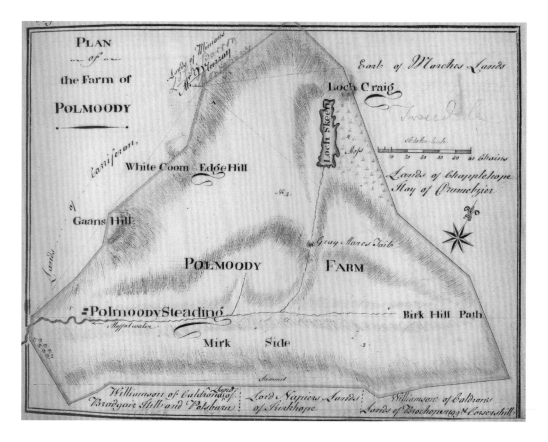

Polmoodie: the estate map after the 1767 plan.

a long time. There is just enough left to catch the eye of the romantic and conjure up for him Wilkie's painting of *The Cottar's Saturday Night* or David Allan's *Penny Wedding* or document the less happy scenes from James Hogg's story in *The Shepherd's Calendar*, of 1829. But the truth of all such events can be found in the raw, set out in the parish-by-parish records given in the *Statistical Account*, which first appeared in 1799. Each was written by the minister of his parish and covered all of Scotland. The accounts followed a set pattern but within it they varied according to the temperament and literary skills of the author as well as in length and complexity. Many read like an extended sermon, some made more cheerful reading than others, a few such as that for Ettrick, just across the hill from Polmoodie, set out a grim picture worthy of Hogg at his most pessimistic. In such an account, the Ettrick valleys were collectively described as possessing 'no advantages' for their luckless inhabitants, especially when none of the landed proprietors was resident, and where 'for many months' there is 'no intercourse with mankind' at all. It is no small wonder that Hogg's grandfather talked to the fairies.

The parish accounts evoked in their different ways a fading and lost world that disappeared irrevocably with the agrarian reforms of the 1750s. It was at this time that the Annandale Estate – like many others across the Borders – fell to the improvers and in this case to the Earl of Hopetoun, who built as well as reformed. He saw agricultural improvement as a moral duty and in his restless hands, both men and houses moved forward or disappeared, in much the same way as happened almost a century later during the more infamous clearances in the Highlands. Hopetoun was ruthless in his honourable way, so little of the past remains to spoil any improver's view across the valley. Part of such reforms included the remodelling of the farm at Polmoodie within a web-like system of enclosures and dykes that were in their turn modernised and expanded a century later in the 1860s. Together, they show the adaptation of the landscape to two centuries of hill farming. They also suggest a sort of self-sufficiency, reflected in how the house was built from the hillside stone or roofed with slates quarried nearby as much as in any farming style practised. The dykes and newly enclosed fields were part of the new order of things, all of them a manifestation of the social control of the natural and human worlds characteristic of the eighteenth century. But time has moved on: the long miles of dykes are coming near their end, some collapsed and sunk, others patched with post and wire, and the sheep that voraciously ate men are themselves on the way out. Few of the cottars' descendants survived the change, the rest departed to the New World, especially Canada, while only a handful stayed to work the new sheep farms and manage the stock of the improved breeds. One of the new men, energetic and deeply interested in such sheep, was David Irving who took up the tenancy at Polmoodie in 1787.

Irving's farm was probably not entirely new and possibly shared its site beside the essential, hillside well with a predecessor of some sort. The fanks and sheep pens, set above and away from the house, were certainly on top of earlier enclosures whose outlines and the odd cornerstone are just visible: they no doubt provided the raw material for the nineteenth century building. The stylised map of the farm, surveyed in 1767, shows enough to suggest history of such a kind that may have followed the lines of Ronald Blythe's *Bottengoms*. He wrote 'There are farms which appear to have grown furtively along the wasteland … like a bit of edible fungus on the main family tree' and it was on a similar such spot that Lord Hopetoun and his surveyor may have built. Though the spirit was new and improving, rather than old and traditional, there were none of the grander appendages of the past such as those found at Roundstonefoot or Bodesbeck, where both farms had grown out of small, medieval towers in Blyth's fungus fashion.

From the outset, Polmoodie was a practical and unpretentious building, humble and workmanlike, a machine for a farming tenant, paying between £100 and £150 a year for a ten-year lease. Such a man had crossed the bridge and turned his back firmly on the cottar style of grazing and summer farming and the itinerant life it entailed. Nothing here was intended to be easy and both house and the adjoining farm buildings had a Spartan air that they retained as their neighbours became bigger and grander in the course of the nineteenth century. The house stayed as a sort of doll's house with a simple pattern of doors and windows, rather like the Dr Barnardo's savings box of my childhood, except it was far from pretty. The box house had a thatched roof, latticed windows, and roses round the door and the whole thing painted in bright, primary colours and much nicer than any house I actually knew. For me, it enjoyed a status well above that of a toy. The slot for coins was hidden in the thatch and there was a circular disc in the foundations for collecting the modest savings. It was Hansel and Gretel country, an essay in escapism that only became real when the money bank was opened, its contents counted and cycle begun again. It taught me in a rather gentle way that appearances could deceive and that banks were not all they seemed. How such thoughts were conjured up by a forlorn and dilapidated farmhouse has puzzled me but I think it was such helplessness that took me back to my childish box.

My Barnardo's box came to me when, during the war, we moved en bloc to the safety of Southerness on Solway, a seaside spot, which had started life optimistically as a planned village for coal that was never found. It was a lonely place, constantly threatened by the sea and wind, and defended only by the lighthouse perched on large outcrops of black rock that rose menacingly in front of the house. Our small cottage was simple, perhaps primitive, hidden away and called by my mother Smookey, a play as much on the Scottish word for insignificant as the character of the chimney when used. It was heated ineffectually by calor gas in cylinders and lit by dismal, paraffin lamps that cast long, dark shadows everywhere and frightened the small and foolhardy. In such a place, the Barnardo's box in my bedroom belonged to a different world, a bright and safe one, to which I would desperately have liked to escape – the veritable port in a storm. Something of this lay behind my strong feelings that cottages and savings somehow went together; a sort of admirable frugality that encouraged discomfort. For such reasons, the relatively grand house has never appealed to me beyond a historical interest and those of a lesser, rambling sort, filled with corridors and eccentric heating systems, expensive and impractical, upset my childish taste for regularity and domestic order. I knew too that they were often haunted, with hidden, dark rooms and the like, something I was quite certain was never true of life inside my Barnardo's box. In many ways, it became my architectural yardstick. I was happy when later on it appeared to fit a Bauhaus approach to function and form but only so long as I pruned the roses and shed the thatched roof from my thinking.

The road from Barnardo's box to Polmoodie was by no means a straight one and among the various wrong turnings taken was my pursuit of redundant Church of Scotland manses; a conspicuous piece of poor navigation. Their appeal was obvious. They came close to my need for modesty; they were rarely pretentious or large and, in the case of rural ones, had been constructed with economy in mind. The minister was never well paid but his standing and income could be improved should he farm or rent the glebe, a large field or two that usually went with the manse. Such a sensible arrangement meant that the manse's setting was amongst fields with the parish church and graveyard as its closest neighbours and together they captured a nice sense of history in often quite isolated, even remote, locations. In the early 1970s, the sale of Church of Scotland manses was in full

left: Southerness Lighthouse and the Solway shore.
right: Our cottage at Southerness called Smookey.

swing, following the unfortunate lead of the Anglican church, so that almost monthly at least one was advertised for sale in some part or other of the country, accurately plotting the decline of organised religion. They varied in relation to my Bauhausian ideal; some had suffered from a rare form of clerical *folie de grandeur*, others from a stylistic change that converted the box into a suburban villa, while many had simply lost the glebe and gained the doubtful intimacy of a modern graveyard. They were scattered throughout Scotland and provided plenty of exciting trips across the country, one at least to the Western Highlands where access was only by boat and the church marooned on a further islet. But it was not their setting that finally took them out of my reach: it was price. As the months went by, they belatedly joined the Old Rectory category in the country house stakes and were valued accordingly and alarmingly: they were rural but not rustic, with room for a horse or two on the glebe fields, and a certain dignified presence in the now diminished community. Curiously, the Church of Scotland forbade that they continued with the manse name as – more understandably – they forbade their use as either a pub or dancehall. But for all that, Old Manse or not, their prices climbed almost effortlessly until hitting £10,000 when I withdrew reluctantly and finally.

I was also aware that the appeal of the Old Manse was low compared with its Church of England counterpart for it had few of the nostalgic, literary associations of the sort evoked by John Betjeman at Farnborough or Rupert Brooke at Grantchester. While there was always the social category of 'the son of the manse', it was a rather downtrodden – if not derogatory – term that clung to academic or political figures. What I looked for in my manse was the sense of place. I came across this feeling evoked by the Welsh rectory of the poet-rector R.S. Thomas at Manafon where there was no electricity or gas, no carpets or wallpaper but whose square Georgian rooms were simple, serious and dilapidated. I never found it.

I would like to think that such hair-brained dashes up and down Scotland gave me time to reflect, perhaps settle on a sensible way forward and become a little less prescriptive in my thinking. I had also to keep in mind that I had a family who might not accept uncritically the view of nothing from the windows of some isolated and unheated manse, however bonny. Reluctantly, comfort and convenience had to be added to the ideal equation and this led me to consider the inside of my Barnardo's box, a perplexing or a stimulating blank, according to mood. At first, I felt sure that latticed windows indicated some kind of art and crafts interior, plenty of wood and blue and white tiles, but later it seemed that the few rooms might be simple squares or cubes and frugally furnished – after all orphans had little. Such unadorned spaces of two or three rooms could be fitted together to form the obvious Bauhaus box, painted a basic white that would emphasise 'the whiteness & lightness & leanness & cleanness & bareness & spareness' of the inside. Then, and about this time, I came upon one of my remote manses that settled the matter for good.

The manse had been built around 1820, on the edge of the West Highlands and in a

opposite: Humpbacked bridge at Capplegill from the Moffat road.

scattered parish where the church was a very distant neighbour. It can never have been a rich parish and for this reason the rooms of the manse had survived unscathed and in the early nineteenth century style of parsimony favoured by the Church of Scotland for such remote places. There was little of Trollope's rambling, Barsetshire parsonages here or for that matter the villa character of the suburban manses of Perth or Campbelltown. The plan was a standard and symmetrical one with the minister's study a kind of interloper and set awkwardly to the rear with a large window looking at an equally large apple tree, perhaps to remind him of Adam and Eve and the Garden of Eden. The room had a faint dash of the gothic but the rest of the house was of a pared-down classicism of the meanest sort, rather like Thomas's Manafon – little plasterwork, just a plain picture rail and skirting boards that matched. The doors were of six, fielded panels as were the shutters that flanked all windows to the front and folded neatly into side panels. They still had astragals and small panes rather than the more expensive plate glass, found in easily accessible and fashionable spots. The floorboards were wide ones – about ten inches – and were stained brown and fully visible. The church style did not run to large carpets or rugs to cover them and favoured instead a basic linoleum laid in large squares – smaller ones for the kitchen or store rooms to the rear. The result of all this simplicity was rooms that could have belonged to a Shaker community, empty and unfurnished when we saw them with only the odd, religious print on the study walls as a clue to the past. Ideally, it was how I imagined the rooms of my Barnardo's box but, unfortunately I knew of none to judge.

I am sure that no such anxieties about the character of the interior ever troubled the owners of the farmhouses or occupants of the manses that I came across during my hare-brained travels to find the ideal box. In my version of John Buchan's Great Game, the Church of Scotland and its expensive manses had been replaced by the Forestry Commission with its odd property portfolio. Like the Church, and following much the same short term thinking, it was regularly selling the houses and cottages of the hill farms, which had been bought for commercial planting in the anticipation of the next World War in one form or another. It shared with the Scottish Church a narrow and essentially negative view of the future and had little confidence in rural society's ability to adapt or survive without its heavy-handed support. For such help, a price was to be paid, and the old, rural adage that trees ate men did not greatly trouble the Commission – after all, the alternative was a museum of rural life, a version of the crofting museums of the Highlands, such as Auchindrain in Argyll. But such critical thoughts were best kept hidden and I was quite happy to exploit its folly, at least for the time being.

The enthusiastic scramble around the more remote areas of Scotland was resumed with growing desperation as the housing stock appeared to shrink, the price rose and the legal conditions became increasingly burdensome on what remained. The Commission itself had grown greedy and now seemed to want the cake and to eat it. With the result that anything of value in their eyes was overvalued and even the ugly came with a high price attached. Carving up the land into marketable units – what was termed 'balkanisation' in a curiously historical mindset – led to the formation of some remarkable properties often without either access or prospect and in the path of electricity pylons. Instead of the manse's pleasant cordon of historic church, churchyard and glebe, there was either a forlorn landscape of ploughed hillside and diminutive Christmas trees or vast swathes of Sitka or Norwegian firs, so closely planted that it was often impossible to find or see the house that was for sale. It was Hansel and Gretel gone mad. Whatever views there may have been were now planted out of existence along with any sense of the history of the surrounding landscape.

The houses and cottages seemed to share this feeling of despair. The actual physical condition of many of them was poor, most were in disrepair and some sufficiently so as to be actually dangerous. They easily outmatched the most disreputable manse and a few were offered as roofless and in need, as the Commission cautiously put it, of renovation. Sadly too, they were without much character or any architectural pretension that might have brought them near to the dignity of the manse. Still, from time to time, the Commission came up with the offer of some relatively unspoilt farmhouse and its steading, lost in the surrounding hills, nearly habitable, and left behind as the forest marched

Roundstonefoot Hall from wartime Nissen Hut with Saddle Yoke in distance.

Polmoodie: view of house from garden with Hydrangea paniculata 'Phantom'.

relentlessly in the opposite direction. It was even better when this included a few fields beside the house, replete with broken-down dykes and a wild crop of nettles or rushes. The trick in all of this was to persuade the Commission to sell such buildings and land intact, without any of the cumbersome restrictions or onerous rights of way that its functionaries held close to their bureaucratic hearts.

The very obvious stumbling block in all such negotiations with the Commission was its uncritical love of the conifer tree – especially the Sitka. The bare hills supporting only a scattering of sheep offered the Commission an unique opportunity to change things for the better with blanket planting on a commercial scale. In their eyes, the few hill farms that remained with their decayed system of dykes and stells were a landscape of the past, uneconomical and largely irrelevant to the needs of society as they understood it to be: it was the 'wasteland' of their original thinking. The various foresters I came across were mostly puzzled that I wanted not only a house but control over the immediate view or what remained of the prospect. I think they regarded such an attitude as a form of elitism and rather resented such thinking as both selfish and snobbish and possibly saw me as undesirable as well – a sort of cuckoo in their nest. For the Commission, the landscape was a means to an end, gained through rigorous control of windblow, brashing and the like, which in itself enjoyed a beauty of economy and function. It did not see much difference between the hills growing trees and those growing grass, and the blocks and rides were just a further form of rural geometry, already introduced by the rectangular shelterbelts of the nineteenth century. It never quite came to terms with the historical clock that showed trees had come and gone and that diversity in them, as in people and animals, was the essential, rural balance of well-being.

Unlike the manse, the redundant farmhouse came in many sizes, shapes and styles. In the impulsive search, I concentrated on those that were in the western Borders, a flexible geographic area where the farmhouse usually came with a steading of some sort and possibly cost less than in other, more eye-catching areas. None, however, reached the solid standards of the manse and this was particularly true of the stables and byres that fell very short of the soundly constructed and well-proportioned glebe outbuildings. Most had had been cheaply and disastrously modernised or extended with ugly metal barns that showed all too well the decline in hill farming that had brought things to such a pass. Of them all, the most popular and practical was the Nissen hut of army surplus, sold off after 1945, and widely adapted to a variety of uses apart from the basic one of storage on a large scale. The village hall at Roundstonefoot and that of the next valley at Cappercleuch, both had their beginnings in such wartime wonders and were simply constructed of corrugated iron fixed to a basic metal frame, usually set on a concrete base. They were almost uniformly painted in the traditional farm colour of a vibrant, tractor red that faded over time to something less aggressive and more pleasing. In an odd way, they gave an even more hopeless air to any farm and together with decayed fencing and yards upon yards of rusty wire suggested some former refugee camp – at least to the post-war imagination.

The farmhouse itself was more often than not a variant of the two-up, two-down with a wing added unhappily to the rear that contained the kitchen and scullery with the bathroom overhead – singular it should be said. The rooms themselves were straight-forward and unpretentious; the hill farmer fell several rungs below the minister in the social order of the parish and well beneath the standing of, say, a dairy or arable farmer. Whatever internal changes had been made were fairly basic – often to the point of ugly – and had to do with keeping the farmer, but not the house, warm. They were mostly nineteenth century buildings and in this part of Scotland were built of stone – whinstone or sandstone – coated with a limestone harling in some form or another and painted white or perhaps a pale shade of yellow with a fresh, yearly coat given only when times were good. Such were the bitter choices. At some stage in any hunt an end has to be called, a compromise found between the ideal and the possible, and a bargain struck that kept face on both sides. The romantic role of some architectural knight saving a hapless farm from the engulfing arms of the forest and wicked bureaucrat should be left to others, much richer and more determined.

Armed with a lengthy list of likes and dislikes, it still surprises me that we found anywhere that satisfied such a demanding bill. I suspect that after a while I saw virtue where few did and came to appreciate what the eighteenth century identified as the capabilities of the place in the manner – say – of a landscape gardener like Brown. I am quite clear in my own mind that there was never any love at first sight, or anything like having an architectural crush on some modest, retiring and unsuspecting building. Still, I remained faithful to the memory of my Barnardo's box through thick and thin. But another, quite strange image arose at this time from my reading of Forster's *Howard's End* as an example of architecture in fiction. The house of the title – based on a childhood home – was a brick Queen Anne farmhouse beside a wych elm, 'a comrade bending over the house', which seemingly had been protected through adversity by an extraordinary guardian called Miss Avery. Vaguely as a housekeeper and sometime caretaker, she had sheltered the rooms and garden as the living genius of the place who understood, sympathetically and enigmatically, that 'our house is the future as well as the past'. Such a benign spirit I added to my list.

OVERTURE

I did not live in a tent while I chased around Scotland in search of my ideal manse or farmhouse. There was another and first house that was home. It was a small urban flat, up some steps and along a tiled close to its outer door and it provided just the sort of blast of reality that I badly needed in 1968. It began with the actual purchase that took me quickly and firmly into the world of surveyors and surveys, lawyers and loans, the difference between essential repairs and necessary ones and ultimately the shiny world of white goods. Then came the alarming first night when thoughts of disaster and ruin filled the sleeping hours, did not fade but grew stronger as the grey dawn approached. I suppose it was a rite of passage; stepping away from the safe world of home, school and university and taking on board the difficult and demanding passenger of responsibility for what seemed like an endless voyage. There was another passenger as well, one who had little to say at first but later spoke with a strong voice – that was money. I heard a great deal from him later on and he always took care to remind me that my first love – my charming Dr Barnardo's box – had been one for savings.

This first house was a flat with two bedrooms and a sitting room in Glasgow. The rooms were of a good size and proportion, the planning compact and the bay window of the sitting room looked directly south over the wooded river valley of the Kelvin. It had the nicely evocative but misleading address of Doune Quadrant: the street itself an almost straight row of six, rather battered tenements – no different from many across the city. It cost a few thousand pounds largely because it was on the ground floor – called by the estate agent a raised basement – and on the edge of a difficult area socially. The spirit of my box was in my mind, both financially and architecturally, and the little place caught something of its simplicity and humility but otherwise it was on the lower rungs of the property ladder in all sorts of ways. There was about it a gritty, no-nonsense character that appealed to me at the time. It also hardened my determination that any future house would never be large or grand or in the suburbs – what John Betjeman feelingly described in 1933 as 'the deep pit of speculative building'.

As we settled in, all the usual good and bad fairies turned up but two were there from the start and quickly became our constant companions, never out of sight for long. The first was the city of the early seventies itself. At that time, it still had its social stratification pretty well intact. We were just within the desirable West End, but lived on the borders

opposite: Sheep on an upland hope at Birkhill.

of a buffer zone with on the other side the decayed and poverty stricken Maryhill, where the wrecker's ball was never still or very far away. It was easily captured in one of the scenes from Edwin Morgan's black *Glasgow Sonnets:* 'So you have nothing to lose but your chains, / dear Seventies. Dalmarnock, Maryhill, / Blackhill and Govan, better sticks and stanes / should break your banes, for poet's words are ill / to hurt ye.' More prosaically, it was wryly documented in Oscar Marzaroli's photographs of the blitzed Gorbals and its desperate tenants. Like much of the western end of the city, it had been developed rapidly in the 1870s and our enclave had subsequently become vaguely bohemian in a raffish kind of way, largely because of its leafy setting above the Kelvin. Architecturally, it was conventional enough for its day except that in the middle it changed from Quadrant to Gardens and from tenements to houses, with a decorative railing marking the social transition. In Glasgow terms we were on the wrong side of the track.

The second fairy was the buildings themselves. They were dull, without much charm and on a wet day looked gloomy and even a little hostile. It did not help that they were built in a grey stone, functional without any fuss and poorly maintained like so much of the city, seemingly exhausted by the very act of building. The only attempt to lift their appeal had been the appearance in 1872 of an architectural interpretation of the Giant's Causeway, which led in a double curve from one level to the next as the terraces climbed

left: View into the Kelvin Valley, Glasgow.
right: Blind doorway by Greek Thomson at Doune Quadrant.

the sides of the river valley. The staircase and the elaborate, classical arcading that went with it were attributed – correctly – to the local hero, the architect Greek Thomson. This included the blind doorway at its foot, set into the wall and leading nowhere, like some piece of relief sculpture, which still outraged local feeling of the logical and frugal sort. But, as with so much in the area, there was a hint of the better things that never came, especially when all development died in the wake of the calamitous failure of the City of Glasgow Bank in 1878, whose crash reached even the then tenant at Polmoodie. The descent from dingy respectability into Bohemia had started in the fifties and meant that the old survived where it was quaint and showy or would cost too much to modernise. A remarkable instance of this perverse form of conservatism was the close – in our case an open hallway that led to the stone stairway that gave access to the four floors above. On each floor, there were two flats, each with a doorway directly facing the other in a nosey sort of way. The walls were tiled half way up to protect them from the rough and tumble of close life and as such they were reckoned one up the social scale from tenements with only painted walls: the local term for such refinement was a 'wally close'. The tiles had

Rottenrow, Glasgow, from a photograph by
Audrey Walker, 1955–56.

originally been an off-white but were now dazed and cream and only dimly reflected the gas lights that still lit the hallway as a rather stunning example of traditional conservatism. Like much else, it had ever been thus and throughout our first few years, the Corporation lamplighter came round each evening to light the gas mantle, as in Robert Louis Stevenson's time or for that matter in Ian Hamilton Finlay's poem, *Archie, the Lyrical Lamplighter* – 'not a joke to be an employee / of the Glasgow Corporation'.

The immediate and minute hall of our flat repeated in miniature the character of the close but without the lamplighter. The floor, about five feet square, was laid with encaustic tiles in red and yellow that had fortunately mellowed to something less harsh. Beyond this was an inner doorway of which half was filled by a large panel of opaque glass, engraved with a delicate pattern of urns and foliage, while the walls were covered with a patterned anaglyptic. It set the tone for the other rooms except when some degree of modernisation had slipped in obtrusively. In the sitting room, the grate of a handsome, white marble chimney piece had been replaced incongruously with a small, electric fire of imitation logs while the marble itself was hidden under a thick coat of gloss pink paint. But apart from that, the false shutters of the long, plate glass windows remained, as did the panelled doors and the simple plasterwork of the ceiling cornices. The wooden floor throughout was stained a dark brown and in the kitchen there was a large, indestructible square of linoleum chosen perhaps to continue the desired mood of nineteenth century gloom. It was here that the following century had been allowed to show its hand in the sinks and oven and, in a corner, a large cupboard filled the space that had been the box bed of some minute skivvy, or so we were told. The other flats were much the same and, as many were rented without improvement, time had stood still. There was about the whole tenement a makeshift air, for money was always tight and maintenance sadly confused with extravagance.

A similar spirit was at large on the street outside. Along the kerb that fronted the close, the various parked cars were all of a secondhand sort and provided not only a useful piece of social history but also of car design and colour fashions over a decade or so. Much the same was true when the frontier was crossed into the Badlands of Maryhill. There the streets often lacked cars – even of the decrepit sort – and the odd, bent bicycle skewed across the pavement indicated alone the casual culture of the twentieth century. Such emptiness, with through traffic little more than an occasional trickle, brought out a form of street domesticity where boisterous children drawn from the closes of crumbling tenements filled the vacuum. Once again, Oscar Marzaroli's photographs – or better still those of Audrey Walker – taken around this time and of similar parts of the city, captured a sort of resilence absent on the other side of the social barrier of prosperity.

I don't think that I developed strong feelings about the flat though I did have my favourite room, one of the two that looked into the river valley with its dangerous, after-dark life. It was not large, one wall was window and the other filled by the pink marble chimney piece: it became what was termed my study, pretentious but roughly true, and expected of any academic worthy of his salt. The remaining two walls supported a good crop of books that gave abundant colour to an otherwise white box. At this time in the seventies, white rooms were to be found here and there but were usually held to be both impracticable and silly and in my case – and to my neighbours – shocking – for they were seen as the handiwork of the dreaded and dangerous architect Mackintosh himself. To their way of thinking, such a room belonged in the manse of a Church of Scotland minister, a far from friendly or comfortable place and one of a vaguely reproving nature. I think I made matters worse by having no half curtains or blinds to the window so that the unsympathetic room was seen by all and gained an undesirable notoriety as encouraging local peeping Toms. However, it was reluctantly accepted as typical of the unworldly folly of an intellectual in their midst.

The view inwards was however partially blocked by a large mahogany desk that had belonged to my grandfather, and certainly looked that way all too well. It provided me with an effective shelter from the curious eyes of the pavement audience, always alive to eccentricity in any form and easily amused. It found a friend too in my imagination, easily caught and keen to replace the abstract play of light and shadows, with the movement and impersonal noises of the street and the never far away drama of Glasgow. These made a pattern with a conventional and predictable range of highs and lows – noisiest around twelve and five o'clock – and together they helped to shape the pleasant ebb and flow of

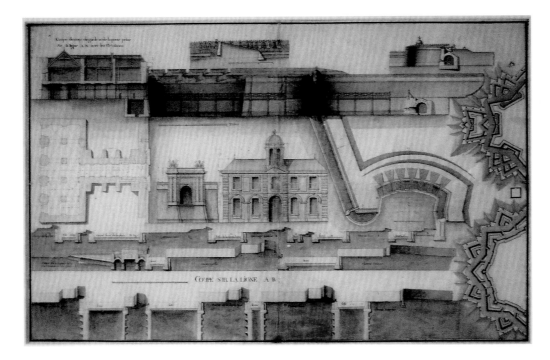

French plan of fortifications of a citadel in mid-18th century from my study.

the solitary workday of turning pages and staring at grey photographs. On the wall and well away from the light of the windows, I had a large watercolour of the stylised design for the fortification of some French town of around the middle of the eighteenth century. Sadly, I have never been able to determine where it was and it may well have been little more than an academic exercise from some military academy or other. The draughts-man was ambitious and keen on detail that extended to the carefully drawn, industrious manikins in regimental uniforms and tricorne hats, carrying swords and muskets, which manned the battlements and guarded the classical gateways. In this conjectured world, there was never a dull moment and all was prepared for an enemy out of sight, beyond the fosse and demi-lunes that the draughtsman had recorded so crisply. Bloodshed and the carnage of war were part of such a scheme of things, all of which made my street scene seem the more sedate and safe.

The other rooms of the flat followed much the same pattern of white walls, wood floor and not much furniture of the comfortable kind. I don't think we ever seriously consid-ered an interior that was in any way historically correct or even traditional, for this would have meant, if our neighbours were anything to go by, brown paint, patterned carpets and fancy overhead lamps, no doubt warm and welcoming but also claustrophobic and in a way defensive. Such rooms were over-furnished, perhaps to offer security and sug-gest a retreat from the rigours of tenement life that was always just around the corner. The firmly closed outer door of an evening meant just that and was a brutal form of do not disturb. We cultivated a different sort of self defence and hid behind walls of books, making a floor-to-ceiling barrier or barricade and suggesting, priggishly, that we had also an understanding and foot in different worlds. As the building block books were largely new ones with as often as not rather colourful dust jackets, they gave life to the rooms and at some point I went as far as to arrange them by colour rather than subject. In such a fashion, we kept faith with our machine for living in and, on the outside at least, we marched with tenement life and stuck with the traditions of community living.

Tenements, such as ours, had evolved in the early nineteenth century to cope with the growth of the city and to house its workers. They were a coarser and cheaper version of the terraces of the century before and remained the only solution to overcrowding until the arrival of public housing at the end of that century. However, tenement living was not for everybody. It demanded tact and firmness and its often arcane rules were part of an unstated agreement that was all about maintenance and maintaining the face of respectability against the odds. This meant that there were strong views on the wash-ing and cleaning of the close, about cutting the grass on the drying green at the back, about pets – Scotties yes but Afghan hounds no – and so on, even into the etiquette of good morning. At heart, it was a fairly sophisticated, informal code for communal liv-ing, perhaps framed for yesteryear, and laid down originally by the landlords who built the often shoddy houses and suggested a better life. It was slowly slipping away and that no doubt explained the acquisition of a tenement flat by the National Trust in the early eighties as an alternative to its endless parade of country houses and castles where life was equally strange and distant to many. The Trust's chosen flat was in a tenement near the Glasgow School of Art and in a more respectable and exciting neighbourhood than ours, but the life they evoked there was a superficial one, just as contrived as their phoney Georgian kitchens where the eggs were never boiled or the ham cut. It was tenement life taken at face value, shorn of the often desperate existence it covered up – the damp, the smells, alcoholism gone – even the standby lucky midden – a Glasgow version of the lucky dip – ignored. Such a flat was unlike those of the working class feelingly – and endlessly – described in the tenement stories of Worsdall and Faley whose books had encouraged the Trust in this direction. To our critical neighbours, it showed how much tenement life, such as theirs, had moved on and how versatile its conservatism had always been and remained.

We had a brother and sister across the close from us who were typical of our sort of tenement life. They were modest, wryly good humoured and would help in any crisis, expect little in return but were sticklers for the tenement code and viewed sternly liberties taken in such matters by more Bohemian neighbours such as us. On the floor above both of us was a married couple with a daughter. We knew and were fond of them but like all such friendships it was contained and bounded by the code – so far and no further – though tolerance was always extended to us for we were the brash colonials from outwith the city. In fact, our past was of little interest to the close and though gossip usually kept such small societies alive and well, it was local, rarely malicious and often funny in a cynical way. The bachelor brother and sister were mildly eccentric and worldly-wise, though neither of them had strayed far beyond the city, except in wartime – for them travel was a closed guide book. Yet, Miss McCairns was a formidable driver who ran the financial side of a small garage empire, and her neighbour above, Mr Menzies, was a car maniac who spent his time under the bonnet, perplexed and exasperated, driven on one occasion to warming the damp engine with burning newspaper. He was safer and more reasonable in his other love, the allotment garden where he cultivated his root vegetables but turned his back on flowers as frivolous. The flats themselves were either owned or rented and such a higgledy-piggledy arrangement caused little friction as far as could be told. We shared a plumbing and heating system where old and new fitted seamlessly together and we were happily united in the adversity of leaks and blackouts. All of this went together with brown paint, linoleum and Jacobean revival furniture that seemed to have formed a collective life and become part of the tenement's character.

Tenement living had its downside. The buildings had been put up cheaply and in haste, so much so that in 1886, for example, it had been possible to build three tenements not far from the centre of the city for £9,000. I doubt if they were built to last in any conventional way or be loved in any other. The coal fires of both the city and Lanarkshire made quite sure that they appeared grim, stark slabs of stone, grey or red, stained and eroded by pollution until the clean air policies arrived in the seventies like some ubiquitous window cleaner. Few architects – apart from those disparagingly called tenement architects – gave their names to such buildings or were remembered by them. Their builders had little need of expensive, professional advice – however sound – in such a familiar and well-cultivated field and rarely took it. As a result, they built following the familiar convention of the copy-cat sort and their tenants were not surprisingly just as undemanding and conventional in turn, easily satisfied with the odd bit of decorative railing or engraved glass. For them, the tenement was their castle, albeit a substantial and rather ugly one and that was the end of the matter.

The Quadrant was set on the steep bank running down to the Kelvin and our particular tenement had a stream, not a burn, below, which kept our flat damp and encouraged outbreaks of wet and dry rot, expensively treated but never eradicated. Its woody seclusion also encouraged our lawless neighbours from across the border and petty burglary was rife but accepted and even tolerated. The occasional disappearance of our cheerful window cleaner was a puzzle until we learnt that he was on remand or in prison and this gave a certain lift to the Bohemian spirit of the neighbourhood – but it was an acquired taste it must be said. The river valley too was disapproved of as a regrettable form of public neglect, while the natural seeding of ash and sycamore, and the less natural one of old prams, bicycle wheels, and mattresses on its eroded banks, were dismissed collectively as jungle. The tenement mind preferred either the functional allotment, such as that of our neighbour Mr Menzies, or the herbaceous borders and decorative cherry trees of the public park, set aside for Sunday outings when the weather was kind.

Much closer to home was the problem of what was to be made of the drying green, increasingly obsolete with the coming of the washing machine and the vanishing of the clothes pulley from the kitchen. It physically divided our terrace from that of the tier above in almost Neapolitan style and had provided space for washing and ball games, tolerated but closely monitored from the windows above. It was also the scene, every Monday morning of washing day, of the informal meeting of the close parliament when the week's affairs were debated vigorously beneath clothes lines and between clothes poles, with the unenfranchised looking on from their windows. In a rather strange way, this simple space, open and functional and very formal seemed to me to have something of the spirit of our flat. So when the parliament debated its future, I was adamant that it should remain as an urban space and not turned into the laissez-faire jungle of the Kelvin valley to which they took such exception. I painted a rosy picture of its immediate ancestors: the small walled garden of the seventeenth century with simple plantings of box and yew and few flowers, held together by its strict geometry, all historically fanciful. But my neighbours were persuaded – almost enchanted – and so too was I. For in my mind, Dr Barnardo's simple box had acquired a new garden, one that swept away the roses from

around the door and dug up the beds of hollyhocks and the like below the windows and replaced them with the geometric drying green of my over-stimulated imagination.

The drying green affair was something of a watershed and encouraged an unfortunate move from the frying pan to the fire. I was offered a tied house by the University, a form of conscience money, for my chair brought in an income of nearly half a million – well in surplus after paying me the going rate. Rather like Doune Quadrant, it sounded better than it was by a long shot. A flat had been carved rather insensitively from one of a square of houses built by Gilbert Scott when the University moved from the steamy heartlands of old Glasgow in 1866 to the airy heights, west of the city. The houses were grey and gaunt in a Gothic style that could be described as economical and were meant for University professors, with whom they found little favour. Number 13 was set prudently beside the chapel and for good measure was usually the home of the Professor of Divinity – the second one at that. In a roundabout way, I somehow thought that this might test my

Looking up the Blackhope burn to Hope Fell.

feelings about manse life without either owning or living in one and whether the atmosphere – modified Barsetshire – was one I really wanted. The rooms within the flat varied
from the too large to the too small and had little of the nineteenth century about them
now, unlike Doune Quadrant. But as we were on the upper floor at the top of the house,
our sitting room window gave an imperial view westward over the city and beyond to the
sea girt lump of the Ailsa Craig. Rather less pleasing was the bell that rang on the hour,
making the less industrious aware of time and its passing. It sounded as well at the beginning and end of lectures – it was the eponymous Hurry Bell of student life. This distant
feeling of mortality became overpowering in the end – it was unpleasantly like hearing
time running smoothly through a jar of sand. It helped put paid to any remaining love
for manse life.

I think we had moved on and found ourselves at odds with many of our neighbours
and increasingly wary of rules and conventions of any kind. I had seen too much of city
life, too deeply, often too close for comfort, and found even the images that Joan Eardley
painted of the dysfunctional Samson family and their grimy, Townhead tenement superficial and trite. After all, we had had the reality of murder on our doorstep – below in the
Kelvin valley – and experienced a police force drawn from the black humoured, detective
stories of William McIlvanney in which crime and Glasgow were synonymous. As relief,
the ghosts of the manses and farmhouses that we had pursued off and on came back to
life and the close-knit society of the tenement and all its edginess faded in appeal. But
the manse was slowly left behind as too expensive and too full of dark corridors ending
in dank pantries and still rooms and with too many heartless, knolling bells. I also wondered if I would not be swapping the duties of the close for those of the former minister
with his role in parish society as the inhabitant of the 'Old Vicarage' or whatever name
the Church permitted for the former manse.

Such a narrowing of my game of houses and ladders left only the redundant farmhouse on the board. Here, the danger was not that of the ersatz minister but of the hobby
farmer, running a few sheep or the odd cow on the couple of acres that the Commission
had grudgingly spared from the tree. It would be hard as well to fit tactfully into a society,
more or less in decline, without perhaps seeming familiar or condescending. There might
also be more than a whiff of the rapacious carpetbagger about our opportune arrival. Still,
though there appeared to be few obvious rules, unlike the close and its code, we needed
nonetheless a guide of some kind who would not upset us or our putative neighbours: we
required urgently the sort of Miss Avery figure that I recalled from *Howard's End*. Such
a person would understand almost instinctively what we and the house needed and fit
us together firmly and tactfully. The trick in all this was to recognise the figure when it
appeared as the guardian of our fortune.

Robert Borthwick, the last tenant farming at Polmoodie, had given up and those who
worked there and at Birkhill had all moved on. In fact, the house when we finally saw it

had been empty for two years and was more or less derelict. The farm had been around four thousand acres in its heyday, a fairly typical size for a hill farm in a remote area, and was now roughly split between forest on the hillsides with sheep along the valley bottom. It was barely a satisfactory or profitable arrangement. The farm – apart from the house – was in the hands of an absentee farmer of cattle rather than sheep, who had little interest beyond paying a weekly visit to have lunch of a sort with his shepherd in Birkhill – weather permitting. All the while, the Commission dithered between retaining the farmhouse, steading and the surrounding few fields or washing its hands of any vestige of farming and sticking to trees. It was also under pressure from the National Trust, who had acquired the area of the Grey Mare's Tail, to respect the historic landscape of the valley and keep as much as possible clear of commercial forest. In the end, the Commission made the worst of all worlds and ended up with three owners and a regrettable exercise in balkanisation where the rise and fall of regimes and shepherds, foresters and rangers was almost on a yearly basis. But out of it all, we discovered our Miss Avery.

We needed someone to help with our quite small children, and who could manage the chaos that surrounded us and them almost permanently. What they and we needed was an anchor and we found our special form of ballast more or less next door, as happens in all the best fairy tales. Mrs Learmonth was the wife of the shepherd at Bodesbeck and had been there for about ten years before we came. She knew both the house and the Borthwicks, our predecessors, well enough, though she had come from the other end of the Borders. This gave her always a certain detachment from the comings and goings of the valley and a growing awareness of its increasing difficulties. As in any shepherding community, she disliked an empty house and even more a farm that seemed to be limping irreversibly into oblivion. I think she was more relieved than surprised when she found the house lights on as she drove up the valley of an evening. She was as discreet and firm with us as with the children, and quick to point out when we were reaching dangerous waters, where the rocks were, and how soon we should don our lifejackets and swim. Though no historian in any formal sense, she understood the inevitability of change and gave the vacuum cleaners and washing machines, cars and telephones a cautious welcome. Her husband was rather less flexible and more conservative, though he had adapted to the agrocat, dipping stick and so on, realising that the valley had moved on and carried him with it, however reluctantly.

The first measure of Mrs Learmonth's worth was apparent at the valley Christmas party held in the corrugated Nissen hall with a local Santa Claus in full rig, handing out presents from the crib and revealing an impressive doctrinal pragmaticism. There was something for every child and Mrs Learmonth pointed out that there was a new baby at Polmoodie and she would, on their behalf, carry a present to him. In this way, we were introduced formally and easily to the community, regardless of any silly social conventions. She remained our guide and guardian for thirty years.

LOOKING

In the seventies, the Forestry Commission sold its properties according to the administrative areas in which they lay. These were termed conservatories and each was run logically enough by a Conservator – a misleading title if ever there was one. The properties it had for sale were nearly always farmhouses or cottages with the odd bits of land left behind from their timber operations. Their sale was advertised in the local newspapers on the weekly property day and apart from local gossip that was the end of it. After declaring an interest, you were sent by second class post a cyclostyled sheet on cheap, coarse paper, written in a manner that managed to be bureaucratic in tone and at the same time vaguely dissembling. It was pretty obvious from the start that the Commission's heart was not in the property business and any agent worth their salt could have done better and more speedily. As it was, the to-ing and fro-ing in this ritual dance was left to the local land agent to conduct and, as he had other and better things to do, you were regarded as a form of nuisance – a tiresome ne'er do well, possibly looking only for a cheap day out. After a while, you learnt to accept your place as a second class citizen and realise that the agent was little more than his master's voice, that the Commission had limited interest in houses or landscapes or the rural community and in some cases appeared to actively dislike all three.

The second entry in the Commission circus was the visit. No two were the same. They all started off conventionally enough with a telephone call that sent you into a twilight world of dereliction and ugliness with some unfortunate forester as your guide who, as often as not, simply pointed the way. Invariably, it was a wild goose chase where the suggested price accurately mirrored what was offered. If it was a small, roofless cottage in the middle of some new conifer plantation the price would be low; the same cottage, but with a corrugated iron roof and the suggestion of electricity, a bit more expensive and so on up the scale until you reached the farmhouse category where hundreds moved into thousands. Quite often on such jaunts, you came across your rivals, sadly a shifty and not particularly appealing bunch of opportunists, who showed, distressingly, a similar but unseen side of one's self. It helped to make the Commission's distant and disdainful approach understandable.

Part of this by now formalised game was meeting the forester on site, usually a somewhat gloomy hut or even just an enclave in the wood. They were a varied lot. Some were

opposite: Some of the Soay flock beside the house at Polmoodie.

devoted to the tree in any shape or size, others were rather bored minor managers, a few were nowhere to be found, while many regarded the whole business of selling houses either as a joke or imposition. There were, however, one or two who were curious, interested in people and happy at the prospect of new and congenial neighbours who might actually stay and make a go of things. One such was Mr Gutch. He was a Warwickshire man, small and lean, greatly interested in horses, hunting, and dogs – lurchers – who had joined the Commission to heal the mental and physical damage of a Japanese prisoner of war camp in Burma, an experience he never mentioned or discussed. He was thoughtful and always helpful, though reserved and often remote, but was, I think, amused by my enthusiasm. When we did move into his forest area, he and his wife were endlessly helpful and seemingly tolerant of most of my opinions and surprising ways. He lived in the former schoolhouse and schoolroom at Roundstonefoot where, until a decade ago, there had been sufficient valley children to keep it going. In an odd way, he maintained the schoolmasterly tradition of the Scottish dominie, a measure of seriousness and caution, and in all of this he was supported by a tactful wife, skilled in jams and chutneys and familiar with most aspects of good husbandry. If I had to imagine a subject that he might have taught, it would have been a straightforward one like mathematics where the answers were either right or wrong.

Polmoodie was on offer with another, much bigger and more expensive farmhouse, possibly one as a foil to the other. They were both described in the flat, unemotional language of the Commission, more or less pitched to discourage all but the most determined day-dreamers or opportunists. The larger farm was in Tweedsmuir, so that the two places were about twenty miles apart and belonged in different forests of the endless conifer; this meant that in the division of labour Mr Gutch controlled only one but sold both. The other difference between the two was that the farmhouse at Polmoodie was to all intents and purposes derelict while its rival was in reasonable condition in the Commission way of things. The asking prices, we were told firmly, reflected this as did their sites – one on the banks of the Tweed, the other the minor Moffat Water, one a fisherman's joy, the other his despair. Both had the customary problem of access, the outcome of the Commission's determination to have its own way at all costs. It was particularly keen on the right of way concept that allowed it or its contractors of any kind to lumber and churn past the front door without warning and also gave its farming tenants extensive rights across fields and through woods. Whoever drafted such sale particulars understood little or cared less about the buoyant market for the hidden retreat, well away from the world and its everyday troubles: friction over rights of way, doubts about water supply, obscure boundaries and their shared maintenance would soon put paid to that. The vaguest notion of *domos placidas* had not arrived in woody circles evidently.

Almost all of such drawbacks were immediately present in the sale of Polmoodie. The house was offered with an arbitrary five acres. How the boundaries had been arrived at, for what reasons or for whose benefit were unclear even to the Commission. The three-ring circus it produced took time to act out and only after some star performances from the encircling farmer and his henchmen was I able to buy a further six acres. This helped to make sense of the traditional grouping of house, steading and in-bye fields, but did not remove immediately the right of way through the farmyard created in the farmer's favour. It remained as a burden on the property for sometime to come. Because the Commission was firmly convinced that I had gained too good a bargain, it would not consider any further deals or special concessions and suggested that I and my farming neighbour should settle down like the biblical lamb and lion and make the best of it. As far as the Commission was concerned, I had bought the proverbial sow's ear and must be content: the conversion to a silk purse interested them not at all.

It was not so much the house as the steading that opened up a storybook. It was a long, low block of roughly coursed whinstone, which continued the horizontal line of the house and contained what had been a dairy, stable, byre and some sort of storage space for wool presumably. It looked as though it had changed little since it was built, though the stable and byre had been modernised inside and the entire roof system had been reslated with small Welsh ones, perhaps not for the first time judging by the dumps in the nearby fields. It was an agricultural palimpsest and not a particularly happy one, which put me in mind of the sad poem by Edward Thomas written in 1916 'Look at the old house, / Outmoded, dignified, / Dark and untenanted, / With grass growing instead, / Of the footsteps of life, / The friendliness, the strife: / In its beds have lain / Youth, love, age and pain'.

The steading also made clear how the eighteenth or nineteenth century farm, for that matter, had been run. The stable had stalls for two farm horses on which a horse tax was paid in 1797. Further along there was the byre for about a dozen cows and calves and somewhere between the two was fitted in a mixture of cats, dogs, and hens. Hay was apparently dried in the wool store after it had been emptied in the early summer. There was also a small pigsty that had been added later to the field side of the steading, which probably held a couple of the animals in the short term. The three large fields across the river provided the hay, which was stored and used to feed the horses and cattle during the long winter months. There was a door that opened from the byre directly into a smaller field that would have allowed the cows to come out immediately after milking. It was easy to see how it all worked for it was a straightforward and simple economy that contrasted with the older, rougher and tougher existence of shepherding on the hills. Much none-theless depended on weather: making hay must always have been a gamble. Now, there was about it all an unnatural silence, an uneasy stillness of which the uprooted trees, broken walls and fences seemed part. The unkempt fields of rushes with crooked corners of nettles and docks suggested, even more forcibly, an abandoned way of life.

Such a spell was easily broken; a few animals, a tractor of some sort, an obedient collie

Overlooking the Moffat Water valley

to do the hard work, a few hens and perhaps a noisy cockerel and the farm would come alive, superficially at least. The trouble was that I was no more a farmer than I was a minister with a large manse and glebe to worry about between my sermons. I had neither the time nor enthusiasm for such a demanding role nor for the rigmarole of milking and feeding at the crack of dawn and in the rain. The solution appeared to lie in simplification: to stick to sheep, the more self-sufficient and biddable the better. There was also a tradition for farming here with sheep of a different sort. *The Statistical Account* of 1794 explained how the tenant farmer David Irving had crossed a form of the white faced Cheviot with the local Blackface sheep to produce a heavier and woollier animal whose descendants were all around me on the hills for better or worse. I did not find them appealing except as walking history books and they were far too rebellious for a place in my or any ideal world. Rather luckily, an alternative presented itself through a book ambiguously titled *Island Survivors*, which appeared in 1973.

Island Survivors turned out to be a somewhat dense and factual account of the sheep that survived on the Outer Hebrides islands of the St Kilda group from which the population had been removed in 1930. The sheep from one of these islands – Soay – had been saved by the Marquess of Bute and a few ended up in a Bute property in Fife a few years later. They had a rich history as the sheep of the Celts, domesticated well before the long tailed variety arrived with the colonising Romans, and had survived happily on a remote

Small Soay lamb about a week old.

and isolated island such as St Kilda. These sheep were much more interesting than what was on offer commercially and became even more so when I discovered that they were both hardy and self-sufficient, needed only a little feed in winter, required no shearing and looked after themselves efficiently and successfully in lambing. My role was as an extra. In contrast with the black and white army, they were dark brown with a pale undercarriage of the moufflon type with white circles round their eyes and bottoms that reminded me of the painted elephants in one of the Babar and Celeste stories. They were also described in a Gaelic song from the neighbouring island of Hirta, which translated as 'the foot of the Hirta sheep, / That was a nimble foot! / That was an elegant sheep! / The colour would grow on her back, / She would need neither lichen or soot, / But spinning the wool to make trousers'. I bought four ewes and two rams from the Fife branch of the family and transported them home in the notorious Ami station wagon from which they enjoyed the view contentedly while causing traffic chaos briefly on the Forth Road Bridge on the way. Neither the Blackies nor their owner was amused.

The broken-down character of the farm no doubt helped the Soays feel at home for they were familiar with the ruinous crofts of their native islands. They may have appreciated the sense of freedom given by the minimal fences and dilapidated dykes of their new home and enjoyed the uncontrolled river that looped around and through the fields at will. It had certainly been an essential element in the farm's character and economy – even in its downfall. It was crossed, just below the house, by a rickety bridge that led to the main fields of about thirty acres, the hay fields, which were divided into three by what had been rather handsome dykes. It was here that the river proper was born from the confluence of three burns that included the major one that came from the old glacier valley at the Grey Mare's Tail, about a mile or so away. The river perhaps saw itself as the older and supplanted rival of the road and one that had set the pattern for travel from east to west long before the upstart Birkhill Path appeared in 1767. Until then, it had been little more than a track, casually linking the cottar homesteads to the summer grazing enclosures. Both river and road had had to cut their way through scrub woodland of birch and alder, which formed thickets with the heather and rushes on the river shallows. So much so that neither can have provided an easy passage for any but the hardiest and most determined of wayfarers. But there was pattern enough for the simple business of moving sheep along the hills or practising some sort of basic agriculture on the scattering of cultivated terraces: the regular traveller had yet to come.

It all must have seemed to the proverbial crow, casually flitting by, that this was a simple landscape of river, road and fields, which fitted happily together and had changed little over the years. The same impression of unity was found underfoot when climbing one of the steep hillsides and finding the rough stones were those of the river banks or field dykes or for that matter the house itself. I had been struck earlier by the same thing when – at the Whitechapel Gallery in 1971 – I looked at the artist Richard Long's walks in the wilderness and read that 'I like simple, practical, emotional, / quiet, vigorous art', and even more tellingly 'I like common materials, whatever is to hand, / but especially stones. I like that the idea that stones / are what the world is made of'. He might well have been describing the miles of dyking around me, some old and some older, and their source in the large outcrops of greywracke and boulders scattered all around like the skittles from some giant's game. They had been used in the rudimentary terracing of the past and later formed mounds of cracked or heated stones for burning, or so the archaeologists rather half-heartedly believed. The several steps to their use as the rough walls of the house and steading were easy to follow and marked a tangible transition from past to present.

As with so many things in this world, change came suddenly. In 1989, the nephew of the difficult farmer at Birkhill decided he preferred the sheep of the Australian outback to his Blackies, hastily sold out to me and departed promptly. And, about the same time, the Forestry Commission decided equally abruptly to sell the timber on the hills across the river that they had planted so densely and diligently with the alien Sitka spruce and larch nearly fifteen years ago. With much misgiving, I bought the forest privately, largely because I promised to make things difficult about rights of way – a trick I had learnt from the Commission of course. The trees themselves were not close to maturity but the accepted wisdom was that they should be felled when around forty years: if left standing they certainly would be blown down and become expensive to harvest. So there was little to be done except wait and pass the time with some remedial planting of sycamore and other broadleafs along the edges and bottom. I was cautioned against my immediate urge to fell the stunted trees at the top to form a more natural skyline: an expensive operation that would leave behind some lunar landscape worthy of H.G. Wells and his *War of the Worlds*. It was made clear as well that I would be expected to replant and in similar density. But time was on my side, for sooner or later some form of destructive tree disease would come along, like those affecting the elm or larch, and the decision would be taken out of my hands. In the meantime, I could attempt, perhaps, some form of land art, modelling the trees to follow the contours and hollows of the hill and the vertical patterns of the dried up burns and stone outcrops. All I needed was courage and a chainsaw, of which I had neither.

The farming operation, however, presented a challenge of a very different kind and in this instance time was not on my side. In the traditional way of farm sales, the sheep stock went with the land and had to be taken on at an agreed price – a variation of the shopkeeper's demand that if you wished the tomatoes you had to have the leeks. The term for such sheep was hefted, which meant that they knew their way around the hills and the grazing cycle of the valley and were superior in worldly wisdom to any that might be introduced to replace them. The irony was that these were the lawless Blackies that had made our early days such a misery and had become hefted to jumping my walls and eating my trees. Part of the deal too was the acquisition of the near ruinous cottage and steading at Birkhill, along with several miles of collapsed dyking and minimal fencing. It was not what I had had in mind when I started my duel with the Forestry Commission and I think no one was as surprised as I was at the turn of events in which a large cuckoo had appeared in their cosy nest: overnight I had become a shadow of the weekend farmer.

I had, with the arrival of the nineties, a hill farm of several thousand acres, a rebellious sheep stock and a less than charming cottage with outbuildings. I was unprepared for such responsibility, for neither manse nor Barnardo's box nor a city tenement flat offered guidance or inspiration and, moreover, I did not need further challenges. But what I did need, and pretty well immediately, was a tenant for the cottage, after it had been put in some sort of order. I made clear that he – no females answered the advertisement – would take on the sheep and make sensible and practical repairs, so that the ranch farming practised by my predecessor and his minions became a thing of the past. This left me with the familiar tasks of repairing the dykes and stells, bracken and thistle cutting, all of which I had tackled albeit but on a minor scale, and dealing with the river and the whole system of field drains that ran into it when working. Standing back and assessing what I saw as a historical landscape, it was easy to understand how the farm had come about and the importance of the river in such an evolution. The pattern of the walls, how they mimicked the river, turning from straight lines into curves as the water had moved this way and that over the last few centuries, was clear enough. Such erratic behaviour had left behind a

View along the river towards the new bridge and new embankments.

maze of elaborate channels and shoals of stone, pointing to the ebb and flow of historical floods and droughts. The crumbling banks and small islands were the remains of unsuccessful banking and ill-fated drainage schemes embarked upon in the more recent years. With better luck, I was about to play my part in this wet and thankless task.

I was given the advice that the best approach to a river problem was to work with it – to go with the flow – and not to confine it by high banks to some narrow channel as had been practised so often in the past. In fact, I should establish a sort of flood plain where it could rise and fall, expand and contract to its heart's content. This was the wisdom of the

River banks and greywracke showing the beginning of the Moffat Water.

local river board – the Moffat Water was a tributary of the Annan, an important salmon river – and they were prepared to back their suggestions with money, if only to prove their assessment correct. I rebuilt the derelict bridge as my part in the scheme and they undertook banking the river to the east by forming a series of inlets of porous steel nets, each filled with river stones, and set at twenty feet intervals to break the flow of the river. Such peninsular-like projections were intended to form pools in which the salmon could shelter and spawn – at least in theory. The wide, sloping banks were built from the spoil from a forestry track, made solid by the heavy wheels of the tipping lorry, and following the sinuous course of the river. The board also generously undertook to plant a scattering of trees – ash and oak – along the new banks. This was done by a rather spirited and not particularly young volunteer group: I was not told until later that those enthusiastic volunteers were from Dumfries prison. On the broad top of the west bank, I made a grass walk of about six feet wide that soon carried a rich crop of heather, harebells and thyme and even the odd orchid.

What remained to be done was to control the river to the west where it marched with my neighbours at Capplegill and Bodesbeck. The key point was an area of around four acres where the river and a hill burn joined forces and flooded – marked on maps as Whitewells Bush. It had been planted as long ago as 1767, possibly with hazels of which a few descendants remained amongst the stunted birch and prevalent rushes. The large field adjoining the river at that spot was flooded several times during the average year when the fishbone system of clay field drains became clogged and it often ceased to work altogether in winter. The major channels of the drains needed to be opened up and cleared and, at the same time, the adjoining river bank raised on top of a layered, stone base to form a gentle slope that followed and repeated the curves of the river. It was a similar plan to what had worked upriver and gave the water sufficient room to expand and contract more or less at will.

All of this was in my mind when I finally started in 2012 to work on the river bank with an experienced digger man, the son of a former farming neighbour who understood the lay of the land as well as I did. It was a serious and technical matter for him and, after general instructions had been given, it became quickly apparent that I was little more than a spectator who should wait and watch: any mention of land art was out of the question. Nothing was easy, the ground was soft and the new bank of one day could sink and easily vanish overnight if there was heavy rain and because of such hazards the pace was slow though relentless. The work attracted little attention except from the all-seeing Environmental Protection Agency – SEPA was their onomatopoeic title – who seemed apprehensive that it would appear ornamental rather than useful and could encourage some frivolous spendthrifts in such ways. The sight of a heavy tractor racing up and down the bank to bond turf to stone was felt to be provocative – too much like fun. When done, I resisted having contractors plant the curving banks and did it myself. I was sure that my amateur planting would have a natural and less regimented look, better to match the irregular forms of the self-seeded ash and sycamore that I had collected earlier. In time, they would form an important shelterbelt to the prevailing south-west wind as well as softening the contours of the banking and make a pleasing silhouette for the setting sun: it worked and looked good and simple and fitted Long's definition – 'A good work is the right thing in the right place at the right time'. It just about fulfilled my wish to display the pleasure of the practical.

In the early eighties, I went with what was then the Fine Art Commission to look at Ian Hamilton Finlay's garden at Stonypath, which had recently become Little Sparta or, as the sardonic neighbours had it, Little Upstarta. The Lanarkshire location was an even bleaker one than mine – a small hill farm gone to rack and ruin, seemingly brooding over its misfortune in true Scottish style. It had been given to him by his wife's family, something he played down along with her creative role in the garden itself. He had remade the setting in the style of a desert oasis and this suited surprisingly well the desolate and dreary landscape of the area. Wisely as well, he had laid out a garden in which flowers were more or less irrelevant and such a prescriptive attitude I could well understand for it was one I shared. But I did not warm to his relentlessly intellectual style and punning jokes – bring back the birch – as well as the garden's lack of a sense of place. He had written about this and about other gardens in the past, and I somehow felt he found gardening to be petty and bourgeois. It seemed to me that Stonypath was a joke at society's expense – after all, Finlay's great hero was the bloodthirsty revolutionary St Just, the Angel of Death – a far from comforting spirit of the place to have around. After a visit there, I was flattered to get a letter from him, direct and unpleasant, that made quite clear that the garden was an aspect of his work as a poet and he was uninterested in the silly concerns about its conservation and future by hangers-on like me. Apparently such letters were not unknown. I came to think of the garden, like the cottage where he held court in the bed-sitting room, as his form of false modesty. He was contemptuous of possessions of which he had few and wanted less; at heart, both poetry and garden were an intellectual game, albeit with modern rules and conventions.

Finlay was not a gardener. Like his sculpture, it was made by others but always according to his plan and with scrupulous directions that left little to chance though he rarely anticipated either growth or expansion. He was keen on humble plants and in his short story *Midsummer Weather*, of 1953, he described the garden as 'a dew-wet wilderness with nettles and tall, firey weeds'. So much so, that he maintained 'A garden of nettles would be eloquent testimonial to Scottish culture', and to its prickly qualities as well. By such floral reluctance, he came near the spirit of the eighteenth century landowners whose parkland, shrubberies and circuit walks followed some iconographic plan, revealed by the inscriptions on temples and urns discovered en route. Something of such a green kind of garden appeared nearer home, just a little north of Dumfries in the valley of the

River Nith, beside the electrified railway to Glasgow, which meant it was neither secluded nor barren like Stonypath. Its innovative creator, Charles Jencks, was, like Finlay, not a gardener in any accepted sense and the philosophy of the garden was for him scientific not literary. Like Stonypath, Jenck's garden was a practical and clever response to a setting and in this case to protect the house – Portrack – from the noise of the railway and the flooding of the river. This was done by making a modified ziggurat in grass and water that took over and expanded several of the themes spelt out in the conventional, formal garden nearby. Later on, Jencks went further and perhaps a little less successfully in response to needy railway repairs and turned part of the track banking into a selective and national Valhalla – a railway station for the Gods as a Post Modern aesthetic. He repeated his idiosyncratic grass and water mounds in front of the Gallery of Modern Art in Edinburgh where they acted once more as a noise screen to the road as well as asserting on a national platform that the city too was a piece of sculpture.

Both Stonypath and Portrack were bold variations on landscape themes that left me far behind. While I had hopefully seen the end of commercial forestation for the time being, it was now left to me to manage the damage done as best I could and with limited resources. My small plantations of beech and sycamore would always be minor themes within the two miles or so of conifers, clothing the hills from top to toe; though they may have softened the blow, and given a little historical sense to the landscape. The work on

Moorland view of Stonypath and its landscape setting.

the river was possibly the more successful for it kept its winding freedom as well as the character of pools and channels while ceasing to be a perennial headache. Though change may have been managed to an extent, it had happened and certainly any former tenant returning, any Johnstone or Gibson, would not have felt at ease, happy or at home in the new setting of his old house.

In this, I was unhappily reassured by an account of life on such upland farms in the sixties that appeared in the introduction to the Galloway and Borders volume of the *New Naturalist Library*, published in 2007. Its author, Derek Radcliffe, was a botanist in the widest sense and had known Polmoodie for a long time, in fact since 1949, when he carried out his research here on peregrines and ravens. His visit was on the eve of the wholesale forestation of the upper valley that he so vehemently opposed and detested. He rented a room in the house for most of the summers of the next twenty years, along with a similar arrangement in an upland cottage in Kircudbrightshire. In his book, he illustrated Polmoodie from the west with the sheep fanks in the foreground and in the distance the bedroom window of the upper room where he usually stayed. He wrote nostalgically in his introduction of 'the good times I spent staying with shepherds and their families in lonely places among the Galloway and Moffat Hills. They were some of the happiest days of my life, returning at night to wonderful suppers and good talk'. He was deeply grateful 'for their kindness to a young man with a bicycle and pack'. Barely a decade later, the way of life he had seen was over, gone along with the empty and bare landscape to which he was devoted. For our part, we had Mrs Learmonth, our Miss Avery, who had survived all the changes that had befallen the shrunken shepherding community and now discreetly helped us to fit into what remained.

opposite: View to the west from Derek Radcliffe's window at Polmoodie.

SUPPORT

It has doubtless been written somewhere, and cynically, that any house is as good as its builder and even better when there is no architect. I had no architect at Polmoodie until much later in the day so hopefully something of this may have come true. My first assessment of the house was as a simple geometric block – little more than my Barnardo's box but in need of basic restoration. It offered me a suitable opportunity to apply Venturi's rigorous definition of architecture as 'shelter with decoration on it': the situation was certainly sufficiently bad. Shelter was needed for the roof had large holes in it, the doors and windows were far from watertight in any practical sense and much of the rest of the house was infected with spectacular dry rot. It was only when all of this was out of the way that I could turn my hand to Venturi's 'decoration' and in this I made an odd, initial choice. Above the window of the porch, I fixed to the wall the lead badge of Royal Exchange insurance company, number 221136. It was probably of the late eighteenth century and showed the rather handsome elevation of the earlier building in London. Its purpose had been to make sure that when the fire fighters turned up they read and expediently checked badge and policy before turning their attention to the blaze in front of them. I had in mind the feeling that such a lead badge would again act as sort of talisman, possibly in the spirit of the yew or ash tree that supposedly gave protection from evil, and could provide shelter for the house by some Pictish divinity or other.

For all this work, my builder was Mr Schoolar. He was a friendly but formal man, always in an old fashioned suit and waistcoat, whose firm, Alexander Schoolar and Son, had been established in Moffat in 1913. It was to last for the next seventy years: he was the son but sadly without successor. I found him sympathetic and always helpful and, once he had my measure, I was allowed to give on-site directions to his joiners and builders, as well as to have the run of his builder's yard. His local network extended to electricans and painters whom he briefed on my behalf and to whom – I suppose – he vouched for my credit. If this is too ideal a picture, there was a flaw, he had little sense of time and was always one job behind and that was invariably yours. An interview with him in his office recalled a visit to the confessional where you were heard with understanding, the future deftly sketched out and you emerged relieved and hopeful, foolishly so of course.

Once Mr Schoolar had you in his net, you were allowed unrestricted access to his yard, a graveyard filled with the skeletons of local houses. It had at its centre a wartime Nissen

opposite: Bill Hean's Wellingtonia from Threave Gardens.

hut of some size which stretched to housing often large parts of buildings, so much so that it seemed time itself was kept and slept there with building history persuaded to stand still. There was apparently no particular logic or sense about what he stored or how it was arranged, and much of the stock that remained there had been either too heavy or too inconvenient to be thrown away. Amongst all of this, I found my panelled doors and shutters, the odd cast-iron chimney piece, red sandstone flags and box guttering. But better still, I enjoyed my time, enlivened by the thrill of this sort of architectural chase. Mr Schoolar also had an ally in the painter running the local firm who, from time to time, as Schoolar fell well behind in some critical job, stepped in with an extra pair of hands or two and was even found both digging and plastering well after five o'clock on his behalf – such was the Schoolar charm or desperation. It was the same painter who told us that as an apprentice to his father in the late thirties, he had cut his teeth papering the back stair of the house with a baleful red-brown wallpaper that survived until our day. He was saddened to see it go; his past thoughtlessly and ruthlessly stripped off and replaced with plain paper that required no skill beyond patience. The nearest he ever came to revenge was when his son, over-enthusiastically burning the old paint from a casement window, set it on fire brightly and briefly.

Mr. Schoolar's personality rubbed off on his men. He had his trusted stalwarts who stuck with him through thick and thin. The more thrusting and ambitious ones did not stay long for they saw bright lights beyond Moffat where the speculative building trade paid good money in the short term at least: the feckless simply faded away. I was allocated a reliable pair of joiners whom he judged – correctly – to match my temperament and taste. It was an odd partnership, a sort of double act, based on the solution to the practical problem of transport where the driver dropped off the non-driver at his job and continued to his own. It was repeated in reverse at five o'clock. In this way, I got the non-driving Martin, who was collected and left by the mechanised Jimmy, engaged on a further Schoolar project two miles away. It worked well enough, and in this daft way I had their collective experience for they discussed each job as they shuttled to and fro, along with the foibles of their clients no doubt. Both men were coming near retirement age, firmly set in their ways and, because of the apprentice system of their youth, were a walking compendium of fifty years of craftsmanship. Of the two, Martin was taciturn, rather severe looking, made few comments and ended most discussions where any deviation from the traditional form of panelling or skirting was proposed with his favourite phrase 'just not done'.

Jimmy Wilson became our joiner after Martin Taylor retired. Though shy – he always took a step backwards when asked a question – and a bachelor, he was also a car enthusiast and his great pride was an E-type Jaguar of the sixties that often appeared at weekends, washed and polished, and put his car rivals in the shade. It was of course never used for work. It was he who presented me formally with a George II halfpenny of 1730 that had been discovered when the floorboards were being taken up downstairs. He and the builders saw this as a ritual handing over the keys in some form or perhaps the passing of the parcel of responsibility. Part of his acute shyness took a form of nervous exhaustion that often laid him up for a week at a time under the guise of some health ailment or another, much to Mr Schoolar's head-shaking and vanishing deadline. But he was a sound and diligent joiner, always with a bit of pencil behind his ear, and he took our house and well-being to heart.

Compared with such a pair, the builders were a rough lot, solid and rather characterless, a bit like the concrete blocks of their trade. They had a grudging interest in masonry but a great respect for the surrounding stone dykes and were curiously puzzled that they had stood so long and looked so well: they had seen little of it in the building trade. But unfortunately they all shared the Schoolar interpretation of time, flexible, with tomorrow always just round the corner and never to be approached in haste. So long as this was understood, work moved along smoothly and on occasion they were willing to be pushed if the apparent urgency was explained to them; it was a bit like a worker's collective. Their remaining companions were the plumbers and electricans who took in their stride the antiquated pipes, leaking gutters, meandering wires, dangerous sockets and the like, which existed rather than worked throughout the house. There was nothing new or efficient about the various systems except, possibly, the stone septic tank at the bottom of the garden into which everything flowed from under the house and demonstrated an opaque simplicity that took the hardened plumbers' breath away. The same fundamentalism was true of the electricity that had arrived at the house in the fifties, at the end of two miles of cross-country poles that finished with a flourish in a transformer, set like a giant lollypop beside the house. It was an eyesore and I had the last lap of wiring put underground to the consternation of the neighbourhood and the horror of the electricians, who warned of some kind of volcano in the near future. They need not have been alarmed, for the power was always weak and the light it gave cast a dim and yellow glow as though the house was lit by candles.

All of this was fairly straightforward, well within my competence and the workmen's understanding. However, the eradication of the dry rot that affected the roof and floor joists throughout the house was altogether another and more sophisticated matter. It was the fashionable disease of the period no old house worth its salt could be without – yet even the hint of its possible appearance could sabotage any sale. It was talked of in whispers for the bill was always a considerable one and the cure far from guaranteed: I had already met its more reasonable brother, wet rot, in Glasgow. For all that, the workmen were a strange lot who had mastered the jargon but not a great deal else and rather enjoyed the impressive mushroom like growths that had appeared in Polmoodie during its two empty years. The conventional cure prescribed was a fairly drastic one that involved cutting out the diseased timber, hacking off the surrounding plasterwork, spraying with a petrol smelling, wood preservative and forming a toxic box as a border between the sick and healthy. All of this was directed by a specialist surveyor of a sort, who at the same time employed the technicians to do the work – an outstanding case of the judge and jury syndrome. As became clear later, all that had been needed was the removal of the infected timber, making the roof watertight and the roof space well ventilated, then time and fresh air would do the rest. It was an expensive game that the technicians appeared to enjoy and they lived happily in a caravan parked in the yard, enjoying the country air and view, so much so that they even enquired about the fishing on the river. The end came swiftly enough when they asked, tactlessly, if they could take photographs of the work in progress for a coloured brochure that they were producing. It was not the type of architectural fame that I sought and the caravan departed.

As the house started to take shape under Schoolar's men and after the hasty withdrawal of the dry rot team, I started to tackle other, less pressing forms of dereliction, especially the decaying system of dykes that ran to miles. The key to the problem was obviously an experienced dyker – not an amateur one like me – who would share my practical interest in the past. As ever, Mrs Learmonth had the answer, a retired shepherd Geordie Rogerson. He had often worked with her husband, was keen to keep his hand in one way or another, and probably accepted dykes as the next best thing to sheep. The only snag was that he lived in a cottage nearly seven miles away at the Moffat end of the valley but fortunately close enough to the school bus route. Like Martin the joiner, he did not drive but managed to become a permanent extra passenger on the morning and afternoon school runs up and down the valley. The driver liked the gossip he freely supplied, though the school children found him rather intimidating and an obvious brake on their school chatter. He was a widower, probably in his late sixties when I knew him, and he wore incongruous thick, black framed specs that made him look like anything but a retired shepherd. He was talkative – for a shepherd – always to the point and expressed himself in strong language as though dealing with a recalcitrant collie or a perverse sheep or indeed me.

He worked on building the roadside dyke that was to replace a broken down fence that had become necessary when the public road, which bisected the holding field in front of the house, was formally designated the A708 in the 1920s. Part of any shepherd's duties was the maintenance of dykes and stells, and this meant that he could tell a weak wall at a glance and from a strategic kick the length of its future. He had a feeling for old stones and liked handling those from the derelict walls nearby, knowing by touch what went where. I was the dutiful barrowman in all of this, carting small and large stones laboriously to the site and at the same time learning the ropes. Quite soon I was familiar with cap stones, through stones and heartening, the importance of a smooth batter, and that only amateurs used hammers. For further reading of an evening, I could turn to Rainsford Hannay's authoritative guide to dyking, especially in Galloway, which gave me some theory and history with which to soothe my bent back.

opposite above: Geordie Rogerson at work dyking without specs.

opposite below: A Rogerson wall of 1976 at Polmoodie.

Birkhill looking towards the Grey Mare's Tail with the Birkhill Path beside the dyke.

Geordie had known the house and farm in its decline and viewed my restoration with a wary eye: he had seen it all before with the rise of the weekend cottage culture that had spread everywhere in the affluent sixties. He shared with Schoolar's men an admiration of the workmanship of the dykes and was especially fond of the march one that marked the boundary with Bodesbeck and rose straight and sheer, up and over the skyline. He claimed that it had been built around 1900 by men who walked daily to the job from the next valley, about three miles away as the crow flies. It was quite a tale and one that I only half-believed until I found out that the dyke had been largely rebuilt after the First War when minor drove roads still existed in the area and one had passed there: he was more or less right. Like so much of the wall system around the valley, its origins lay in the dyking mania of the late eighteenth century that linked one century to the other.

On a slope below the house and above the river, there was a small rectangular garden where the walls were in a similar state of decay to the others. A large and old sycamore had been blown down here and its huge branches had broken the walls in an almost regular pattern of wilful destruction. The effect was like some enormous bonfire all set for just the right fifth of November conflagration. The garden hiding within and beneath all this was divided neatly by a privet hedge, now of almost tree like proportions, with the top part cast as a formal arrangement of lawn with box edging. The lower one had been given over to vegetables and soft fruit, but was now possessed by nettles and colonised by wild raspberries and the sky-high flowers of bolting rhubarb. It was not particularly attractive but it was traditional and directly descended from that described by the various Gibsons –tenants in the early nineteenth century and perceptive commentators on the locality – copies of whose correspondence remain in the house. The letters written around 1816 suggest a garden style that can be later seen in the old photographs of the garden at Bowerhope, a farm further to the east beside the St Mary's loch. In that way, it had a horticultural legitimacy or some sort of provenance. Still, it was hardly my style of gardening but with the warning about the spirit of the place, I sought to make order out of chaos and was fortunate to have in all of this the advice of Bill Hean, who ran the National Trust's gardening school at Threave – not too far away. Better still, it was his kind of gardening.

The Threave school was located in the traditional walled garden of a nineteenth century house, a red monster masquerading unconvincingly as a Scottish castle, which set the tone for the plants raised and cuttings taken as part of the Trust's training scheme: the surplus was sold to the likes of me. The only snag in this arrangement was that my garden walls were low, about four feet, and it lay in a frost pocket at six hundred feet that meant even the hardiest of his plants suffered severe shock on arrival, a few malingering but never for long. Like any teacher, Hean was keen to encourage and I experimented with the stalwarts of Victorian gardening, such as the giant Wellingtonia or Monkey Puzzle, as well as plenty of yew for he liked the formality of clipping and its decisive pattern making.

opposite: Polmoodie's lower garden with the three evil beeches.

He was also anxious that I tried the less conventional members of the obvious: he sold me the shrubby Lonicera syringantha and the evergreen Daphne pontica – all still alive and happy – well ahead of Lane Fox's *Better Gardening* credo of 1982 with its attack on what he saw as boring gardening.

Paying for all this was never easy or simple and though funds were available as grants they were always selective and came with an inordinate amount of small print requiring patient attention. Of such paymasters, the old style Department of Agriculture was never an easy one with rules and regulations that seem to have been cast in concrete of the reinforced kind. It also had an unfortunate attitude to the past, it simply wished it gone. The Department was collectively of the upwards and onwards school and this included a fair measure of discreet, social engineering. The response to any claim varied and each inspector had reasonable power to interpret the rules according to the situation as he saw it. They were never enthusiastic about repairs and much preferred to subsidise a new wire fence rather than fund the repair of a dyke or, worse still, justify on paper such a foolhardy decision. To them a concrete slab road or well drained and lit yard was much superior to any existing, cobbled concoction, however practical, and here we parted company. The Department had a love affair with new materials, slick and artificial, which excluded the old ones, such as stone or cobbles, and even cast-iron and slates had little purpose or place in its blinkered eyes. The bright, modern farmyard, properly roaded, drained, electricified and well lit, was what it sought with a determination verging on the belligerent. But it was just possible to strike lucky and find an inspector who had some sense of history and even feeling for a place and who had not been browbeaten by regulations and submerged in paperwork. Later, the wind changed, and in the eighties the Department belatedly discovered conservation and was surprised and disappointed to find so few traditional farm buildings or dyke systems remaining when funds were available to spend generously on their repair and upkeep. The other bureaucratic twin, the old County Council, which looked after housing and planning and had a reputation for being dilatory and unhelpful, was the reverse and contributed handsomely to the Schoolar bill.

The destructive sweep of the Forestry Commission up the valley had left several dislocated farms in its path. One such was Roundstonefoot. It had been a sheep farm of similar size to Polmoodie, but with better land, and had been bought and planted in the fifties with the farmhouse and steading sold off separately. Its owner when we arrived was Dr Wilson, a chemist who had run the chemical giant – ICI – installation outside Dumfries, and who was now a determined grower of vegetables, always ready well before the general run came on the market. I think he saw it as the scientist's revenge on capricious nature. His wife was on the other side of the garden fence, interested in a burnside rock garden where the plants revelled in the alpine conditions and whose numerous offspring were handed out at the drop of a hat to all. Both gave practical advice: his was usually of the negative sort – days too short, ground too cold, plums sometimes, apples never – all remarkably general for a scientist – hers was always much more positive and encouraging – everything should be tried at least once. He had little time for the Forestry Commission and their conifer monoculture, as he frequently explained to Mr Gutch, and waited grimly for the ecological disaster that he knew, and rightly, was bound to be round the corner. But, like many prophets of doom, he was kind and sociable, and both of them took us in when the uproar from Schoolar's men became too much for the hardiest improver. They were at that curious stage in married life when they had started to look alike – his and hers corduroys and distressed pullovers – and where domestic warfare had turned to comedy. They usually put on a good show when we appeared, disheartened and dusty. At the same time, I realised that their cosy lifestyle and narrow world without too much responsibility was not for me, appealing though it appeared; it smacked too much of the Old Rectory style of things or the culture of the weekend cottage. I felt, smugly, that any house or vestige of the farm should work, keep faith with the past, have some kind of communion with the present and not slide into the role of the pretty Barnardo's box.

Roundstonefoot was about three miles away on the same side of the river as Polmoodie. On the other bank and well away from the road was Bodesbeck, another of the original farms but older than most, built on the hidden site of a medieval tower. A little further up was a much earlier, Bronze Age settlement, laid out just above the river, and so the

Shepherds clipping at Bodesbeck, Peter Learmonth on the left.

farmhouse was likely the third in the line of succession. It had too a cave on the hillside that was the supposed home of Hogg's *Brownie of Bodebeck* (the traditional spelling) and so held considerable literary interest. It was a sheep farm where Peter Learmonth, the husband of our Mrs Learmonth, was the shepherd. He was something of an anachronism, perpetuating a personal style of shepherding, on foot with dog and whistle, tweed cap at a jaunty angle, long, shapeless overcoat, almost certainly the uniform of the past. The Learmonths lived in the old farmhouse, his gaffer having surrendered to the suburban mentality and moved to a modern kit house well away from the old steading and the chaos of the yard. I would meet him from time to time when I returned Mrs Learmonth home, another non-driver, from her morning stint at the house. The boots neatly set at the doorway told me he was home from the hill.

Short and thickset, he shared with Geordie Rogerson a kind and modest temperament, always to hand if there was trouble of any sort, car stuck in the snow or sheep needing emergency dipping. On the other hand, he followed the past uncritically, was suspicious of change of any kind but at the same time well aware of what was happening around him and the threat it posed to his way of life: the crisis in hill farming left few or little unscathed or untouched. He had watched the expansion of the Commission on the heels of the breakup of the Annandale Estate in 1963, and had seen Sailfoot, Roundstonefoot and Craigieburn all quickly disappear beneath the conifer blanket with Polmoodie's fate hanging ominously in the balance. And though he moved reluctantly with the times, he had no great love or understanding of the past with all the hardships he had had to shoulder. For him, the old Bodesbeck farmhouse was 'done', the square of steading buildings 'useless', the clock could not be put back – why should anyone bother to try. Along with such changes in farming, there were the social ones. The most obvious was the disappearance of children from the valley and the closure of the school at Roundstonefoot. This was marked by the sudden appearance at his road end of a bright, red telephone kiosk, serving both motorist in trouble and children who had somehow missed the school bus to Moffat. In the light of all this, I think he viewed my arrival with mixed feelings – a further instance of the writing on the wall – and probably wondered how long we would last.

As he became older, Mr Learmonth found the daily ascent of the hill at first light a strain and so a rough track was made for the first leg of his climb upwards. It was on this path – to a lambing shelter – where he collapsed and was taken off the hill by helicopter, ironically for his first flight. He survived but died a few years afterwards. He was pretty well the last of the traditional shepherds in the valley and indeed the end of a line that stretched back to those in the reformed farms of the mid-eighteenth century. The various circular stells that dot this end of the valley are his and their monuments.

The stells themselves – where they survive – made with the dykes a striking pattern over the hillsides and along the valley bottom. The distance from one to another marked out a day's droving for shepherd and sheep, and gave the flock safety at night or refuge from a

opposite: A ruined stell above the house with a larch plantation.

storm. Built for the most part in the early nineteenth century, they are sometimes nearly four feet high, usually circular, and enclosed a space of about thirty feet with often two or three walls extending outwards rather like the blades of some lapidarian propeller. Such walls offered shelter for the sheep from a capricious wind blowing from the west and buffeted backwards by the hills. The stells's location was usually fixed by the end of a day's grazing along one or other side of the river and depended on the season. Most of them had as well a small wooden gate that could be closed when the sheep of a particular hirsel were rounded up to be kept safe overnight. They were the flock's centre of gravity and marked out the grazing area and the amount of time that could be spent there according to the shadows cast by the encircling hills. Such high hills were largely for the summertime when the sheep driven there would be cool and comfortable, free from the plagues of midges and tick that drifted along the valley bottom. It was a simple existence, free of shepherd and shepherding, with only the odd stell built on the more accessible parts of the high ground and near a water source. Just as well, for the maintenance of the curved walls of such stells was an essential part of the shepherd's duties and never an easy one, especially on high ground. A hilly farm, not too far away in Ettrick, ran to fourteen of them by the end of the nineteenth century and this was not exceptional. Even on a relatively poor farm, such as this one, at least six had been built on the lower slopes of the valley bottom. Two of them were large, relatively elaborate in design and incorporated small lambing pens, tucked neatly into the walls, which were square for once and

View towards Bodesbeck Law with Moffat Water in the foreground.

composed of big and awkward boulders, rolled rather than taken from the nearby outcrop of greywracke. It looked for all the world rather like a steading in some miniature farm.

Such then were some of the leading players who acted out parts in this quiet little drama along the way. It was probably a comedy at heart, cast in yearly episodes, and eagerly watched by a patient but not uncritical audience. As in all good plays, a variety of characters have appeared, some possibly more sympathetic than others, but no real villains or few real crooks that I noticed anyhow. The actors too seem to have grown into their parts as the years have gone by, their roles expanding with time and then – often – simply fading away like the proverbial good soldier or joiner. This was obviously true of the Schoolar workforce from which Jimmy Wilson saw us through both our improvements and his lifetime. Mr Gutch too has moved to forests anew and no real successor has appeared: the Commission has become in part the Forest Authority and so both job and house have gone. The latter has returned, in title at least, as The Old Schoolhouse, a variant of the Old Rectory, but distinctly distant from any rasp of the dominie's blackboard or the dusting of his chalk. The often infuriating Department of Agriculture has vanished too into a clutch of new names, along with the easy-going and often perplexed inspectors, disconcerted as much by their masters in Dumfries as by us and our puzzling ways. The drama that they and others had concocted for us has become a historical one with action limited and subdued, closer perhaps to an over-long, domestic farce and no doubt a little on the dull side.

OLD BOYS

All houses have either heroes or heroines who from time to time pull them from the brink of structural or aesthetic disaster. There are also the more humdrum figures that guard the building and guide it through difficult times. And here we had in Mrs Learmonth our Miss Avery figure – kind, watchful and discreetly on hand. But the biggest enemy for all such buildings is improvement. Luckily and largely, Polmoodie escaped the fate that befell most of its neighbours in the valley who grew in size and wealth but not in beauty. History shows that the farmhouse of 1767 probably lasted with little alteration until well into the nineteenth century when it was modernised and cautiously improved but in no great style and always mindful of expense. The interior's outstanding monument to conspicuous consumption, the curved wooden staircase – a rustic version by the estate joiners of that in John Adam's Moffat House, begun in 1761 – remained untouched together with a few wide floor boards and six-panelled doors. However, the roof was raised to make a proper upper floor and in the process the dormer windows and chimneys were heightened and increased – all of which was the handiwork of Robert Johnstone, tenant in the 1860s. The long, adjoining steading buildings survived externally at least and gave height and rhythm to the house as well as sharing the same colour – white. The farm then went to sleep with the agricultural depression and only in the early 1930s were porches built to the front and back of the house and a few odds and ends undertaken; not so much an awakening as a turning in its sleep. Telephone and electricity came later and not long before our arrival.

The immediate setting of the house, isolated within a circle of trees at the bottom of a long valley, clutching its dykes and buildings closely to itself, has not changed a great deal. Over time, the farmhouse had become a modified T-shape rather than rectangle and at some point an attempt was made to form a front and back entrance, suggesting a clear distinction between the farmer's house and the shepherd's bothy. As part of such social engineering, the original door disappeared, walled up within an outside lavatory, until found in the renovations of the seventies. In its place, the new entrance was marked by a small porch with a larger one stuck on to the garden side of the house for good measure. This was fed by a ridiculous and diminutive driveway from above the yard that ran through double entrance gates to the door, the whole thing worthy of Gulliver's Lilliput. Oddly, the same thing happened at the next door farm of Capplegill, possibly around the

opposite: The march dyke between Polmoodie and Bodesbeck, rebuilt in 1923.

same time, but with a better and more stylish sense of competitive folly. I removed gates, drive and porch in a simple exercise in putting the clock back.

On the yard side, I rebuilt the porch and gave it a doorway with a fanlight above, divided into three in the traditional style of the south-west. I also made the door a fairly sturdy lined one and so well able to take care of itself come what may. In front of it, there had been an arc of cobbles centred on the old front entry and laid to keep the hungry sheep from the door. It had been overgrown by grass and moss of various sorts with the odd outbreak of stonecrop, which I now rolled back easily and found that the cobbles below had been laid in a simple but pleasing Y-pattern: again I was putting back the clock. The remainder of the yard was covered with small, grey stones, taken from the river, which needed deepening and thickening to keep down the weeds. The colour of both stones and cobbles gave me the grey tone that I used for painting the various yard doors and the window surrounds of the house. It was several shades lighter than the mottled blue of the roof slates but they all came together in a rather satisfactory way.

This could not be said of the yard itself where the long block of stable and byre simply petered out as it ran in a slope towards the red Nissen barn. It had been fiddled with to fashion at this end a garage with cumbersome double doors that contrasted with the other smaller ones, barely more than five feet high. I replaced this with a new garage, using old slates and with an old, very rusty skylight from the Schoolar yard set into the roof for

The yard at Polmoodie from the reconstructed garage.

authenticity. It was at right angles to the wool store and together put an essential visual stop to this end of the yard. The timber work inside was open and here Jimmy Wilson followed diligently the pattern of joists and rafters of the old building and gave it the feel of some medieval tithe barn, though a damp one. To one side of the garage, I built a dyke and beyond it planted hedges of hawthorn so that together with the steading they formed an enclosed space. The remaining gravelled area was just wide enough to allow the postman's van to turn with due caution. Unhappily, this reorganised yard seemed more defensive than its predecessor, the door somehow less open and welcoming, the whole much more formal – too organised. There was at this time a rather ridiculous children's poem, popular with mine, by the American Shel Silverstein, which caught this whiff of a one man show: 'A house that's meant for privacy, / A house that's meant for peacefulness, / A house just meant for only me. / There is no door where strangers knock, / No window where they peek and grin. / A perfect keep-out house … / Now … how do I get in?'.

Silverstein was right: the yard I had contrived was out of step in all sorts of ways. It placed a not very subtle barrier both physically and psychologically between the house and the visitor, the very opposite of the traditional open welcome of country life. Much of this was a response to the change in the road above the yard. It had run in the past through the original holding field for the sheep – in for clipping or dosing – then served as the Birkhill Path for Sir Walter Scott and his carriage, but was now the busy and noisy A708 with its share of accidents and arguments, linking not so much farms as towns. We had become part of a roadside show to be casually stared at during a boring journey

Polmoodie from the road in 1973 as we first saw it.

from here to there and possibly seen as little more than some minor relic along the way. Altogether, it made me rather fond of Silverstein's 'perfect keep-out house'.

None of my predecessors would have understood or tolerated such a reclusive attitude; they were always keen on company of which they had little enough. After all, it was from a party at Polmoodie in 1793 that Robert Burns' Jean Lorimer of Craigieburn eloped to get married so disastrously at Gretna Green – the home of forbidden weddings – and live unhappily ever after. And it was possibly around this time that one of the tenants Robin Laidlaw appeared in James Hogg's stories 'gathering the Polmoodie ewes' around Loch Skene at the top of the Grey Mare's Tail, along with Tam Linton, his herd at Birkhill. According to the story, Laidlaw later 'went on to the Highlands and grew a great farmer' – probably accurate enough for the Laidlaws were Hogg's cousins. It seems likely that he was followed by the more definite and historical figure of David Irving, who took up the tenancy in 1787. He was host to the memorable party in 1793 and was succeeded in turn by Thomas Gibson, a further characterful figure. But as far as the house was concerned, it was Robert Johnstone, who spanned the middle of the nineteenth century as tenant, and set his seal firmly on the buildings and landscape.

Apart from such names, the one event that appears to have caught the local imagination and given identity– certainly to Birkhill – was the devastating winter storm of 1794. Hogg's *The Shepherd's Calendar*, of 1829, used as narrator an old shepherd to recount storms as far back as the seventeenth century, all of which paled before that of January, 1794 when 'snow lay from the middle of December until the middle of April, and all the time hard frozen'. It was known as the Gonial Blast, where gonial meant dead sheep. When it was over, virtually all the sheep stock in the area had perished together with seventeen shepherds. Hogg maintained that the storm was at its worst in the area from Crawford Moor, south to the centre of the Borders, and this would certainly have included the eastern end of Polmoodie where Irving was the tenant. He singled out in his story the night of January 24th as the worst, when 'all at once with a tremendous roar that I imagined it was a peal of thunder until I felt the house trembling to its foundations'. Hogg then added thoughtfully, 'that night a child might understand / The Diel had business on his hand'.

Such malignant catastrophes were more or less cast as the background to shepherding life and put in perspective the risks run by the likes of Irving or Gibson on a hill farm during winter. Hogg made much of the changes that had taken place in farming and landowning since the middle of the eighteenth century with the arrival of fresh faces from the north and west as part of the new broom. He felt certain such reforms had hastened the decline of the old families such as the Lintons, reduced to shepherding at Birkhill. He was of course describing the effect of the agrarian revolution where on large estates, such as those of Annandale and Buccleuch, new farms replaced the old cottar way of life and new farmers such as David Irving took the place of the casual graziers with their summer flocks. These had gradually given way to different breeds of sheep, such as the

New Leicesters, developed by the pioneering Robert Bakewell of whom Irving was an enthusiastic and dedicated follower. He wrote in 1791 to the chairman of the Board for the Improvement of British Wool, Sir John Sinclair, setting out a succinct account of his breeding improvements, where he had more or less crossed Cheviot with Blackface, and his climb up the farming ladder. He explained that he had started out on two adjoining farms, Waterhead and Macknaw, both in remote and bleak country between Boreland and Eskdalemuir, in the eastern end of Dumfriesshire. He stayed there for eight years but 'being young, and without much experience', he was soon in trouble, probably from lack of capital, and moved to a similar, possibly cheaper farm nearby at Black Esk Head, where he continued with his breeding ideas. Then in 1787, he boldly crossed the range of Moffat Hills, about twelve miles north as the crow flies, and descended into the valley where he took on the lease of Polmoodie on the Annandale Estate and stayed for a decade.

He was in time to be settled in and more or less ready for the storm of 1794. As one of the estate's remodelled farms, developed by the surveyor William Tennoch, it may well have taken his imagination with its reformed air of well-slated newness and bold system of enclosures that gave him 138 acres of arable ground. According to the *General View of the Agriculture in the County of Dumfriesshire*, of 1812, good houses and good farms went together and if a suitable tenant was to be found then the rent had to be justified for 'men of capital were not willing to live in hovels', a hardly original insight into property management. An acceptable farmhouse was characterised as 40 feet long, 15 feet wide, and 8 feet high, which meant that it was single storey with some form of glazing set into the roof. It was not a high standard and one that Polmoodie clearly rose above, making a startling contrast with some of the unreformed farmhouses immediately to the east. Such buildings were described as 'thatched, small and low roofed – a room at one end, the kitchen at the other, and through the kitchen another room, generally used as a bedroom, with perhaps two small attics above, reached by a trap-ladder, and lighted by a few panes through the thatch'. An establishment, such as Polmoodie, encouraged a fresh outlook on farming and seemed as well an appropriate home for Irving's crossed breed of sheep, perhaps brought with him when he moved earlier from Black Esk Head. In all of this, he was one of the new arrivals of whom the conservative Hogg had so heartily disapproved.

Irving's sheep stock on the farm ran to 1,410 Blackface ewes and he successfully crossed a thousand or so of them with the woolly North Country Cheviot rams. According to the record of the farm given in the *Statistical Account*, this policy had doubled the value of wool produced and raised the price by more than a third, though such figures were given during the good times of what was termed 'the French wars'. After 1815, the pattern changed fairly disastrously for hill farming and continued to do so as the luckless career of his successor Thomas Gibson showed. Hogg's narrator described how in 1823 such men 'have lost their summer day during the French war, which will never return to them; and the only source they have, as I can see, is to abandon their farms in time, and try to save a

The hill fanks from the road in the low autumn light.

remnant … stocks of sheep are fallen so low, that if they were to sell, they would not pay more than the rents, and some few arrears that every one of us has got into'. His logical conclusion was 'as to hanging on at present rents, it is madness'.

Hogg may well have had Thomas Gibson in mind for it was a close community and he was not too distant from his Border farm at Mountbenger. Near home, Hogg had also the distressing example of some of his Laidlaw cousins who left Ettrick en bloc for Canada in 1818, under some charitable emigration scheme. Gibson's weary account of his affairs in the same year spelt this out clearly: 'I have endeavoured to show (and I think plainly) that the present failure has been occasioned not so much through rashness or bad policy as some may be apt to suppose but through a cause of unseen losses which it was impossible to prevent being lost since the farm was taken'. This was a reference to the high rent agreed with the Estate when he entered the farm and the future looked rosy and profitable. The possible explanation for his difficulties was his slowness to read the writing on the wall, adjust his relatively sophisticated life style, and return to the Spartan self-sufficiency advocated by Hogg where, 'you have your sheep, your cow, your meal and potatoes: a regular income from sixteen to thirty pounds yearly, without a farthing of expenditure, except for shoes; your clothes are all made at home'. In his homily, Hogg had the needs of a shepherd rather than a thrusting farmer in mind, and he was attempting to invent an enviable but unlikely past. He would have had little sympathy with Gibson and his silver watch and status as gentleman farmer.

Thomas Gibson followed hard on Irving's heels and both tenants had the standard nineteen year lease, typical of the newer farms, which also made some allowance for the improvement of house and land. He may well have been interested in breeding too for by 1834 it was noted that most of the sheep in the valley were Cheviots, 'only a few black faced breed are left in the most exposed pastures, and a few crosses of Cheviots and Leicesters in the lower farms'. Both men seemed to have shared a similar disposition, able, intelligent, anxious to move on and make something of themselves and the farm. More is known of Gibson because several of his family letters, and a few to him, have survived for the period from 1811 until their departure in 1818. The picture was a happy one and reflected an energetic and comfortable existence in the house, even if the farm was moving into troubled waters. There were seven siblings, of whom the eldest was studying law in Edinburgh and the youngest at boarding school in Yarrow: all showed some interest in books, particularly of the practical sort, as well as the garden and local travel. But all this came with a price that cannot have helped the economy of the farm already burdened with improvement costs, especially in dyking both there and at Birkhill.

Dyking was a mania from which few farms at this time escaped. Since 1786, several miles of such walls had been built throughout the valley, beginning with the lower farms of Craigieburn and Roundstonefoot, with the encouragement of the landlord where the farm was rented. The cost was not great at 7s. 6d. for eighteen feet of dyke in 1812. In most cases the labour was from the farm and the stone for the dykes themselves came from the fields they were to enclose. They were expected to last several lifetimes if kept in repair and they did, even where circumstances had changed. A fair instance was the march dyke between Polmoodie and Bodesbeck, so much admired by Geordie Rogerson, which climbed in a straight line from the river to the summit of the hills, rising over a thousand feet. It seems to have lasted well enough until 1923 when it was rebuilt by a pair of Moffat dykers, Geordie Boyes and Tom Gracie. It was a single rather than double dyke, without the necessary support of through stones, and so was of a weaker construction, but even this stood the test of time.

The census for the Moffat parish of 1851 gives a factual description of the valley's inhabitants from Birkhill at the top to the seven lower farms. Of them all, Capplegill was the largest, and the census recorded that its tenant James Johnstone employed fifteen servants, working sixty arable acres and grazing three thousand of pasture. At Polmoodie, there was Robert Johnstone, aged 39 and unmarried, who was given as farming 4,000 acres and employing 4 shepherds, with at least one female servant in the house, in addition to the two shepherds, William Scott and Robert Walker in the bothy. There was a further pair at Birkhill, one of whom, John Broadfoot, was married with two daughters and who, apparently, could always be relied upon for 'good homely cheer, and a hearty reception from the gudewife who might sing'. It is possible that the two Johnstones were related, though it was a common enough local name and there was a further one at Hunterheck, a farm just beyond Moffat, in 1851.

Robert Johnstone was still at Polmoodie in 1862, according to the *Postal Directory*, and remained there until 1878 at least when his name as 'of Polmoody' appears amongst stockholders of the newly bankrupt City of Glasgow Bank. Like most farmers in the area at this time, he was reasonably prosperous as had been his recent predecessors. According to the *New Statistical Account* of 1834, such men by 'means of skill and capital, with lands of sound quality, and flocks of an established character, are enabled to pay large rents, to employ many servants and artisans'. In Johnstone's case, in the 1860s, he was building on the hard work of both Irving and Gibson, indeed so much so that he was listed in 1863 as amongst the 'farmers with rentals arising from lands in the parish exceeding a hundred pounds', as were nearly all of his neighbours it should be said. This suggests that he had sufficient capital and was adventurous enough to take advantage of the new techniques in farming and his development of the steading and enclosures above the house showed something of such initiative. At the time, there were more than enough books around to encourage such improvements on any scale and one, Stephen's *Book of the Farm* of 1844, with further editions in 1852 and 71, explained in simple and dry language how the new farms had much in common with the new factories beyond their gates. It used its many illustrations effectively and gave designs for the traditional hill stells and brought them up to date, as well as explaining how good transport could or should improve livestock prices and encourage production even in hill country. This possibly lay behind the rise in value of farms such as Polmoodie where the county Valuation Roll for 1871/2 fixed its worth at £950 – not bad when the bigger and grander Capplegill was assessed at only a few hundred more. All of this reflected admirably the era of High Farming, high spending and optimism, all of which came to an abrupt end in the land depression of 1870. But in that sad and long tale, hill farms were perhaps less immediately affected than arable or diary ones, but it was only a question of time before they too followed the rest down the economic slope.

Hand in hand with this general slump went the disaster of the Glasgow Bank whose ripples were felt all over the west of Scotland and where Johnstone had an above average holding of £1,600, probably built up over the good years. It was not a risky venture in any way for the Bank had been sound; its failure put down to astonishingly bad management rather than anything else. It had also spent unwisely on a new and large building by a fashionable architect in Queen Street at the heart of Glasgow, which opened in the year of the 1878 crash. In all of this, he was not alone in the Moffat area for another Johnstone at Auldton was similarly involved with the bank and had also been an investor in High Farming and its expensive buildings. Still, it can hardly have come at a worse time for Johnstone: he was 66, and the money possibly represented his savings and would have brought to an end any idea of further improvements in house or land. He was gone shortly afterwards. Matters may well have been made worse when the owner of the Annandale Estate was declared insane in 1877 and his successors showed more interest in Ireland than Scotland. This was the high water mark, for little that followed was of much consequence and any hill farmer struggled to keep going, let alone find a fresh and profitable role in the new order. After 1915, Polmoodie slipped further down the farming scale and was merged with its Capplegill neighbour for a time. And so, like much of the rest of the estate, Polmoodie went to sleep and was only jarred awake with the sale of the hill land in 1961.

Some work however was done on the house in the thirties and a rather rudimentary plan and elevation has survived to show what was proposed and what existed. It was a basic piece of work, in pencil, and largely concerned with domestic drainage, but it did give a clear picture of the Johnstone house and what had been carried out before the 1878 crash. A bedroom, probably a maid's room, and a scullery had been added to the kitchen and the house extended into the yard. More ambitiously, the roof had been raised and the slates replaced with uniform Welsh ones, the chimneys rebuilt, leaving the old like ghosts in the attic, and proper dormer windows installed instead of the eighteenth century ones squashed below the eaves. On the garden side, a new window had been added to the kitchen – now our dining room – and the bothy made into a separate house with a door to the yard and even its own little garden. Looking at the inept drawing, it is possible to see the move from the all-embracing farmhouse with its inclusive family to one where roles were more closely defined. The style of the interior reflected this with comfortable and fussy rooms of picture rails and cast-iron grates contrasted with the practicality of the adjoining shepherd's bothy.

Nothing of any importance, architecturally anyhow, happened to the house after that and the last tenants – the Borthwicks, Radcliffe's host and hostess – and their three children lived in only part of the house with the bothy empty, unused and barely watertight. There was only one shepherd employed and he occupied Birkhill. This human contraction was matched by the decline in the animal population outside, where the horses and cows were given up along with the making of hay in the summer to feed them. What had been the smooth pasture fields across the river were turned into rough grazing and given over to sheep. Almost symbolically, a garage was formed at the end of the yard, fashioned from part of the wool store, and further along petrol and oil drums were stored in the stalls of the old stable. The house itself became closely linked to its neighbours – and to the Moffat shops – by road and power lines and soon it acquired a telephone number with, rather humiliatingly, Bodesbeck as its exchange name.

The farm had prospered intermittently under its three, resourceful tenants – Irving, Gibson and Johnstone – and what can be seen today is their hard work and resolute confidence in the future. They do not appear to have been men who cared much about the past and relied on their own practical judgement of what could be changed, and what left well alone. They were not always right, but as tenants they were not bound to live with their mistakes and could depart, leaving others to pick up the pieces. Sheep were their way of life and trees of little interest, planted only as dubious protection for house and animals. They would not have understood commercial forestation and certainly not on such a large scale where exotic conifers like the Sitka spruce were harvested and turned over every forty years and the cycle begun once again.

PIECES

Most people – or so it is said – start to collect coins or stamps or birds' eggs as children, that is if they have any form of acquisitive streak or enjoy the euphoria of control. If they continue and develop a taste or compulsion to acquire in depth then the way ahead leads irrevocably to places such as Walpole's Strawberry Hill or Beckford's Fonthill – the magpie's nest on a grand scale. Luckily, I was never a serious collector and my interest in stamps normal, even dull, for I showed little curiosity about their history or geography or even about the particular event they commemorated so lavishly. Later on, I was taken by the thrill of the chase, the primitive hunter's instinct, and found in the sale and auction rooms the battle ground that satisfied my lust, more or less. I became fascinated too with the arcane world of bidding by hand or eye, reserves and increments, view days, catalogues, and by the rich jargon of the dealers and runners who congregated to the rear of any saleroom. In fact, I was often keener to bid than to buy. In my later teens, there were still plenty of small, local auctioneers around who held weekly sales and who, from time to time, branched out to a house or minor country house sale. Such events were often the highlights of my summers in the fifties and offered in their way a salutary lesson in the history of collections and the rise and fall of collectors.

My father encouraged all this and would quite happily pick me up empty-handed at the end of some, often distant sale. I think he saw such events as a useful introduction to the real world of trade, an understanding of the value of money and the management of risk on a small scale. Certainly there were sufficient pitfalls and warnings around, and the auction regulars a strange bunch too, often part of a clandestine bidding ring. Most were the owners of small, antique shops of which every town had several but some were the runners for the bigger dealers in Glasgow or Edinburgh, who used them as their local eyes and ears. There was too the occasional decayed gent, turning his hand unsuccessfully to buying as well as selling the family silver, who was often helpful and kind, and sadly no more worldly-wise than was I. Around them and at every sale was the Greek chorus, idle and noisy, spectators rather than actors, and out for the day.

My coming of age in this world took place in the small town of Dalbeattie, near to where we spent the summer, and shortly before I went to university. I got there by bus and then walked though puddles and rain to a villa-like house, shrouded in the mist and half-hidden by dank trees, a good day for a bargain. The auction was underway when

opposite: Polmoodie from the west with Johnstone addition of the 1860s.

I arrived and there was no sale catalogue, so the small crowd followed the auctioneer, drifting from room to room of the rambling house in a sheepish fashion. It was rather dull. The house can never have been a light one and was now in shadow, the furniture piled into strange and ill-sorted groups where everything was for sale, even the pots and pans and great stretches of baking paraphernalia. My interests were broad and driven by chance but I was taken with a set of military prints and several shelves – they were sold that way – of well-bound books in the small library. The wily auctioneer kept his audience by mixing the good with the bad, making sure that the last lots were of particular interest, with the whiff of a possible bargain for the hopefuls, of whom there were plenty, if they stayed the course. The furniture was much as expected – large, lumpy monuments in red mahogany – and it was matched by runs of predictable magazines such as *Punch* or the *London Illustrated News*, which almost hid the more interesting books. The prints sold well, and so beyond my means, but the eighteenth century books were another matter. They were offered indiscriminately by the shelf with the sets often broken between two, and in this fashion Rollin's *Ancient History*, of 1789, in ten volumes – my goal – was split. I bought the two shelves that included several extras of no interest to me but, luckily, a dealer who had missed them needed them badly, and his desperate offer paid my book bill. I felt very worldly-wise, almost part of the camaraderie of the saleroom, a rite of passage in its way.

Largely for reasons of caution and frugality, my collecting has always been modest, the smallest and most humble of sales usually offered sufficient drama to keep me happy until the next. My collection grew slowly. But as it gradually expanded, my curiosity was roused by how such an accumulation could become a collection and the need for a core to keep it together and give it shape and purpose. I was interested too in the way a holding was set out, indeed often surprised with what went with what and whether an historical or aesthetic arrangement was followed and how rigorously: I never accepted the traditional museum practice of ruthless chronology where changes in technique or taste seemed predictable, even inevitable, and history a straight line.

At university, I had a tutor who was a musicologist and as a bachelor lived in his College rooms where he displayed lavishly on the walls the instruments of his trade. He was especially keen on outlandish wind pieces and trumpets, set side by side or above and below, creating an extraordinary and distracting backdrop to whatever tutorial he attempted in these rooms. He never talked about them and you were left to draw your own thoughtful conclusions in true academic fashion. There were of course plenty of conventional, book-filled studies to be found in Cambridge with a scattering of paintings, old and new, which had probably not changed much in the last twenty years or so as fashion passed them by. But my largely conventional taste was uprooted by Jim Ede's cottages at Kettle's Yard, which offered a radical interpretation of the intellectual interior. The rambling rooms and their contents were open to the interested every afternoon with Ede on hand to guide and explain informally and unhurriedly. His friend the poet Ian Hamilton Finlay described it wryly as 'The Louvre of the pebbles' where a group of stones could be set below a painting by Ben Nicholson. It did not last long and, sadly for many, it became a gallery museum in 1966 and the worse of the conversion. But it had shown plainly what could be made of a small collection and, I think, encouraged my sly trips to the London salerooms, disguised as work in the Reading Room of the British Museum. This led to an encounter with the Soane Museum, just a stone's throw away in Lincoln's Inn Fields, where its founder – the ambitious architect of neoclassicism, Sir John Soane – had lived, had his office, and set up his Museum in 1833. He was precisely the opposite of the gentle and Christian Jim Ede. Soane had arranged his vast collection of architectural fragments around the lower floors of a conventional terrace house that was described as 'still as a tomb, at the bottom of a sea of fog,' and possibly more accurately as '*Non domo dominus, sed domino domus*' – where the house masters me. Around this time too, Mario Praz's book on interior decoration, *The House of Life*, appeared in English, filled with provocative and baffling opinions such as 'surroundings become a museum of the soul, an archive of its experiences', and the more devastating statement that 'collecting is no more than a development, a degeneration of the need to project an atmosphere around oneself'.

In the very early sixties, Soane and his museum were still rather a mystery to all except the interested few. His extraordinary concoctions in the museum of the Monk's Parlour or the Sepulchral Chamber were fair instances of the uncontrolled imagination – a professional version of William Beckford's contemporary extravaganza at Fonthill of about the same time. Still, I rather liked what I saw and following Soane's lead I collected timidly both classical and gothic fragments of which there were still plenty around. This was the period when restoration was a hit or miss affair, where once the old had been copied, accurately enough, it was casually discarded or destroyed, even from buildings of architectural distinction. Behind much of such thinking was Ruskin's dictum that restoration is destruction. A fair instance of this was brought home to me with the purchase at this time of a late Romanesque capital from some French church or other that had been part of such a casual process. On the top of the stone was painted in red the numbers 7996, showing where it had come from in the building and where it was to be replaced. For good measure, there was added in black and at right angles L 996, a mistake that can hardly have made things easy later on. This was a rare find for me – it was mounted and on a metal base – and so had been valued at some time in the past, whereas the great majority of my acquisitions came from some rockery or monk's grotto or had been fashioned into a bird bath and left to decay in peace. However, I prudently kept my fragments indoors, like Soane, though only one – part of a finial by the architect Alfred Waterhouse of 1875 – found a practical role as a lapidarian side table. In all of this and unlike the famous snapper-up of unconsidered trifles, I had little space so that making any grandiose acquisition from some demolished country house, such as the odd portico or triumphal arch, was outside my range.

I was less fortunate in the more conventional worlds of collecting pictures. I don't think my heart was in it somehow. I was not interested in finding a Rembrandt under a bed or anything of that sort and it was a far too professional and competitive world for an amateur like me to fish with any confidence. My earliest and possibly most successful acquisition was a small, half length portrait by a Polish artist Liebeneski, dated 1725, of whom little was known. I came across it in the attic of a local saleroom I frequented and it had apparently been left unsold after some minor auction then forgotten. I could easily see why because it was unframed, very dirty and the sitter a remarkably ugly man: the auctioneer was more than happy to settle for a couple of pounds. After a rudimentary clean with cotton wool and turpentine, what emerged from the grime was a small, stiff figure wearing a captivating, blue dressing gown with gold sprigging, set in a formal landscape

of terraces and balustrading, all in excellent condition. Such success was followed soon by a relative disaster, brought about by my being too clever by half in true amateur style.

In 1959, I bought at auction in Edinburgh a big, lively painting of a foxhunt, not in the best condition, and attributed to the prolific painter of such scenes, John Nost Sartorius, about whom I knew little nor how much his work should fetch. I think I had in mind his famous Earl of Darlington hunt, of 1804, as doubtless did the auction cataloguer in making the attribution. The sale went well and with little competition I was successful. I then set about its restoration, foolishly spending the difference between what I paid and what I optimistically though it was worth. In this, I was encouraged by a friend who rehabilitated seventeenth century ceilings for the National Trust and wished to move to greater and less tedious things. He did just that and my pseudo Sartorius emerged from his easel as a twentieth century fake, imposed on the body of an attractive hunting scene, dated 1845, but with the signature almost scratched out. He photographed this extraordinary hybrid scene where one emerged from the other, the horses with the eighteenth century legs of the hobby horse variety but with bewhiskered riders in mid-Victorian hunting gear. In the end, the rather battered canvas was returned to the full 1845 period and now hangs in the dining room. I don't often tell the tale.

Oddly, my great enthusiasm for the saleroom did not extend to the antique shop. The fifties and sixties were the great period for this phenomenon and no town was without at least one or two, though the quality varied naturally. The Old Curiosity Shop style of

A finial of 1875 by the architect Alfred Waterhouse from Cambridge.

clutter did not appeal to me greatly and I was always suspicious of the owner or his assistant with their obsequious or confrontational manners. Unlike the saleroom, there was no underbidder to give confidence and often no fixed price either, apart from one plucked from thin air to suit the occasion. My wariness in such matters started early, in fact when I was about fifteen and had a few pounds to spent, saved from summer gardening jobs at home. For some wayward reason, I was determined to buy a pair of side chairs of the late eighteenth century, very provincial, rather battered and in elm, I think. I agreed the sale with a small jockey-like owner called Lewis and it was settled that they would be ready in a couple of days when I should pay for them. My father intervened. In the past he had had rather shady dealings with Lewis that advised an unexpected visit to the shop where he found the chairs being glued and having the beetle and worm holes filled with wax and given a thick, surface polish. The sale was cancelled and I was left the fool with more money than sense, for the time being. It took me a long time to recover my nerve and rid myself of the suspicion that the sale room was a more honest place than even the grandest of antique shops. I discovered too that some dealers were quite mad. There was one with a rather dingy shop – more the front room of his house – in Glasgow who was prepared to trade a handsome mahogany chair for my supposed fishing rights on the Kelvin, a tributary of the Clyde, and never famous for its fishing. Even more eccentric were those who dealt in tribal art, which had interested me for a while, and who were described in

1845 Hunting scene in discovery and mid-restoration.

all their nuttiness by Hermione Waterfield in her book, *Provenance, Twelve Collectors of Ethnographic Art*. All in all, I was happier sticking to doing my shopping in the auction rooms and had only perfunctory dealings with that alarming tribe.

There was a further kind of dealer with whom I had a great deal to do during my reworking of the house. This was the type who specialised in building salvage – an up-to-date Border Reiver. Their heyday had been in the early seventies when road and town planners decimated most large cities and especially the tenements of the inner suburbs – a sad and familiar sight in Glasgow. Such dealers, male and female, were a rough and dishonest lot to whom the demolition contractors gave first pickings from their sites in return for some quick reward. The range they had to offer was a considerable one and ran from chimney pots and box gutters to doors and windows and included any sort of ornamental iron or stone work. It was from them that I acquired the gothic cast-iron grate in the dining room, virtually in the nick of time, for Schoolar's men were finishing in the room and the painters ready to start work. To this unsavoury group should be added the opportunists who were quite happy to let you plunder the house or factory that they owned so long as they were paid on the spot and the booty promptly removed. In this way, I bought the William Wilkins marble chimney piece, now in the sitting room: I simply paid the farmer the required five pounds at his new bungalow door and helped myself at the nearby Dunmore Park, a ruined country house of 1822, which he owned and exploited rapaciously. The market for this kind of trade grew and after a while objects started to appear in the salerooms, often broadly catalogued as garden sculpture and dated in centuries, but sad to say that with this gentrification of the trade my contacts slowly disappeared.

It would be quite wrong to imagine that I did not buy things of the garden sort; I did. But in my hunting, I made a clear distinction in my mind between pieces to stay outside and the fragments to live indoors. A wedding present of a stone putto's head, from high up on the grand façade of the Sun Alliance Building in Princes Street, Edinburgh, demolished in 1966, more or less started things off. Perhaps lacking the charm of its Venetian source, it seemed just right for a garden wall, the higher up the better in the style of the original: sadly I never found the right spot or a wall sufficiently high. Still, it encouraged me to look more widely for something happier in a garden setting and away from the feel of an urban one. Inevitably, a saleroom produced two somewhat weather beaten heads in the form of stone consoles, particularly charmless with lolling tongues far too big for their mouths, suggesting some unpleasant form of death, and which unsurprisingly attracted few bidders. They were medieval and had come possibly from some Scottish Tolbooth where executions took place by hanging, hence the tongues, and were intended as an instructive warning to any delinquent spectator. I fixed them to a garden wall, partially hidden, so that they might surprise the unwary, loitering thoughtlessly in a Scottish garden where even peace comes with a price. The cautionary tale was continued by the

A Green Man head from field gate beside the house.

nearby head of a Green Man – the tongue is a tree branch with green leaves – a warning of
some kind though less extreme than the hanging heads. There is, too, more than a whiff
of the old pagan Gods about it all. Apart from these fragments and a sundial of 1735, I
went no further and avoided the expensive garden world of urns and obelisks and the rest
of the ornaments of the formal garden, often trotted in and out according to the seasons
with conspicuous zeal.

By the 1970s, I had accumulated enough of 'my museum of the soul' to worry about
where it should be kept. More than that, I was keen to see how it could be fitted into
everyday life of a humdrum sort. The Dr Barnardo's box was not designed to either hold
or show a collection of even the most modest sort, while the manse might have tolerated a few shelves of books outside divinity, tolerance probably stretched no further and
the Bible was fiction enough. Farmhouses were altogether a different matter and here
the spirit of practical simplicity ruled, for whatever collecting was done was with animals, living rather than dead objects. But at Polmoodie there was the literate, Gibson
legacy and so I could do things differently, so long as I respected the scale and space of
the house and settled on simple things, large or small, set out informally and without
pretension. It was important also that the house kept its domestic air, seemed lively and
awake and avoided the distant imprint of the institutional hand where everything was
'given numbers, fixed to walls or protected by velvet ropes – all is death and the graveyard'.
Such a hapless struggle was part of the character of the small house museum, like that
of Louisiana in Denmark or the Phillips Collection in Washington or of course Kettle's
Yard. To them may be added, as a terrible warning, Mario Praz's own house – a rented and
sunless apartment on the Via Giulia in Rome, 'a crevice of a street like a deep trench', of
which he gave a marvellous account in his book *The House of Life*. In this, he started off with
his entrance hall where he claimed that 'From the moment you enter the flat you become
conscious that you are breathing the air of another age', and the atmospheric immersion
continued through all the five rooms, their Empire furniture and anecdotal pictures to
conclude with the chilling remark that 'I see myself as having become myself an object
and an image, a museum piece among museum pieces, already detached and remote'. The
whole place was truly dead and the title of the book perhaps a sophisticated joke.

In Praz's tour of his Roman apartment, most of the furniture came with a fair amount
of colourful history attached, or so he believed. In my case, there was little to match his
style of anecdotal provenance and the one or two pieces about which I knew something
had no real story beyond the prosaic one of where and when. The elm wood chair in the
hall was typical and its history pretty unremarkable. It had come at some stage from the
Old College that was Glasgow University and had fallen into the casual hands of the
University joiners who used it as a cuddy – a support for sawing – when the old furnish-
ings were scattered after the 1866 demolition of the College. There is an early photograph by the great Annan of some of the interiors before their destruction and several

chairs of the sort were shown in the panelled rooms of the early eighteenth century. It cost me a nominal amount. At the opposite end of the furniture scale is the mahogany and rosewood sofa table with ivory centred rosettes that came from an Edinburgh dealer who often had unconventional things – though always at conventional prices. He was an occasional Catholic who, from time to time, had a crisis of conscience about exploitation and this included his profit margins. His shop was in a quaint, minor street and for security reasons entry was by ringing the bell – never easy for he was very deaf. On some visit, I complained that the prices at country house sales were always high because of the excellent and undisputed provenance of the objects under the hammer. He would have none of it and smartly pointed to a sofa table whose price he reckoned was modest – it was a crisis period – considering its august source. A label glued to the underside, noted in an early nineteenth century hand that the table belonged to 'The lord bishop of Rochester' and was part of the contents of Danbury Palace, a house in Essex, which the bishops used until 1892. There was little more to be said, I bought it.

I doubt if many collectors, large or small, had the same empathy as Praz with their collections. Walpole, Soane, Beckford and Sir Walter Scott were always firmly in control and, unlike Praz, rarely saw themselves as fixtures or objects and kept their distance from the collections that they set out. I am certain that Sir Richard Wallace, standing in the long and magnificent gallery of the Wallace Collection with its walls hung with Rubens,

The Danbury Palace sofa table with ivory rosettes.

Velazquez, and Rembrandt, or Henry Clay Frick in his Fifth Avenue palace, saw themselves as big game hunters regarding their trophies. They were distinct in such a way from the more contemporary Peggy Guggenheim who maintained; 'I am not an art collector, I am a museum'. But what they all shared was a strong sense of control and I am quite sure that they would have fretted over the display of a box of matches. Unlike perhaps Walpole or Scott, such collectors were connoisseurs who gave any object they acquired its chosen space but nevertheless made it part of the all-embracing sum they had devised. The telling of some historical tale was of little interest to them apart from showing a healthy interest in the past and stressing their place in such a scheme of things. The danger was always when quantity replaced quality in their eyes and the setting degenerated into a form of organised clutter, however grand. The path to Strawberry Hill was an easy one and that to the Old Curiosity Shop even easier.

In looking at things, I have always been keener on the objects themselves than their source or provenance and rarely shared Praz's obsessive curiosity about their former owners or status. In much of this, I was a child of the period – the fifties – and my view was decisively shaped by my first encounter with art history that gave a background to my saleroom jaunts. I followed at this time, in a rather half hearted fashion, an academic course somewhat catchily called from Palaeolithic to Picasso. It was set roughly within the framework laid down by the critic Herbert Read when he taught briefly in Edinburgh University during the thirties. The lectures sought to make the case for the closeness of painting, sculpture and the decorative arts and had been derived from his popular book, *The Meaning of Art*, of 1931. I had also come across his *Innocent Eye*, of a few years later, which helped to stretch my mind and indeed eye. It managed in its didactic style to reassure me that my saleroom days had not been misspent and that objects from different worlds and periods could have a lot in common: I was happy to see myself in this way as more of an owl than a magpie. The chaos of the minor saleroom with its exciting and casual juxtaposition of all sorts and quality was a fair illustration of the width that Read had in mind.

There are four main rooms downstairs at Polmoodie, virtually all of the same height and size – that is about seven and a half feet with a floor area of twenty square – one room opening into the other without any corridor. It was a basic plan typical of the smaller farmhouses of the day. Apart from the dining room, all have windows on both sides, east and west, and so the light is even and the direct sunlight, though strong, never lasts for very long. The rooms are painted white, the floors are of plain wood, together they form the box for my collected pieces in ersatz Barnardo's style. The progression from one space into the other is encouraged by the wide floorboards of red pine whose tongued and grooved joints have opened in the course of the years and given a directional arrow from one end to the other, barely hidden beneath the odd rug or two. I have set out along the way objects that are bold of form and colour and so hold and interest the restless eye.

Elsewhere in the house, a similar sort of arrangement is repeated, though upstairs it has become more a game of hide and seek with things half-seen – tantalisingly perhaps – just round a corner and in a different light. Unlike the treasure tours of Praz or Ede, it can all be done in a more perfunctory and less discursive way – perhaps even in less than the proverbial ten minutes.

I have stuck with the inherited pattern of the rooms and the only significant changes I have made have been in the reworking of practical spaces like the hall, kitchen and cloak-room. The form of the house remains the same, even from the outside there can be little likelihood of mistaken identity – it is a farmhouse. But for all that and to me at least, I can still feel the doll's house air and catch the spirit of my moneybox from all these years ago. What is found inside is altogether another matter: here, as Praz would have it, 'rooms are collages constructed connections between the past and the present'. In forming such collages from wider materials than Praz would have allowed, I have been egalitarian; no room is grander or more interesting than its neighbour though their characters may be different. I decided, perhaps perversely, to give my corridor and hall the odd, eye-catcher amongst smaller more modest things and so bring them into line with the weighing of the rooms. The short corridor was the ideal home as well for works on paper for without windows there was little danger of direct light or sunlight. However, no collector is ever strictly even-handed and I have always had favourites who, for one reason or another, manage to catch and hold my eye as they have done for the last forty years. In this way, the story of the seventeenth century Cardinal Mazarin has always appealed strongly: according to the tale, when old and infirm, he would still insist on being taken round his picture collection in the Luxembourg Palace though quite blind.

Map of DUMFRIES-SHIRE from an Actual Survey By W. CRAWFORD. Engraved by Kirkwood & Sons Edinburgh

PEEBLES SHIRE

SELKIRK SHIRE

ROXBURGH SHIRE

LIDDISDALE

ESKDALE

MOFFAT

KIRKPATRICK JUXTA

JOHNSTON

KIRKMICHAEL

WAMPHRAY

WESTERKIRK

TINWALD

LOCHMABEN

APPLEGARTH

HODDOM

MORTON

KIRKPATRICK FLEMING

CUMBERTREES

DORNOCK GRAITNEY

Height of Mountains above the Level of the Sea

Solway Frith

To His Grace, HENRY, DUKE of BUCCLEUC K.G. &c. &c. &c. This Map I with the greatest RESPECT & GRATITUDE inscribe By His Grace's most obedient & most humble servant William Crawford

PART OF CUMBERLAND

CUMBERLAND

PLAN of the Proposed CANAL between NEWCASTLE and MARYPORT

REFERENCES

INSIDE

I was once given, perhaps as a criticism, a book with the intriguing title of *A Journey Round My Room*. It was a flippant account in forty-two very short chapters of the house arrest for forty-two days of an Italian army officer in 1794. Its author was Xavier de Maistre and his confinement was in Turin. Despite the title, it was intended as a parody of the sententious literary tour, given as an account of the interior of his tiny apartment where words more than furniture were to be found. It resembled in some respects the later Praz world of Rome. Maistre barely brought his journey to life and, tongue in cheek, claimed 'the interesting observations I have made, and the constant pleasure I have experienced all along the road, made me wish to publish my travels'. In fact, his rooms formed a large bed-sitter with six chairs, two tables, a bureau and a bed with two mattresses, in all thirty six steps round, and the account was filled out with the feather brained daydreams they apparently induced. He showed little interest in his possessions – they were a joke – none in how they were put together, being altogether more easily satisfied with a warm seat beside the fire or a comfortable one at his bureau. It was a rather fanciful sort of satire.

A more serious introduction to this kind of thing was Jim Ede's account of Kettle's Yard in Cambridge. Written shortly after it became a public collection in 1966, his cottages had already lost much of the immediacy and informality he had guarded so assiduously: sadly, he was aware of the loss. Ede was always able to admire the individual character of the objects he had acquired – often quite simple things – and still see them as part of the collective style of the house, forming what he termed 'the silent influence'. His book also explained his collection with fragments of an essay that accompanied the photographs of the small, intimate groups of his things. He liked the photographs – grainy and in the style of photographer Edwin Smith – so much so that he added the surplus ones to the book as an epilogue, more or less as an end in themselves. He considered them as possessing their own life, being 'the images of rooms rather than the rooms themselves'. His text however was a sharp contrast, heavy with quotations from devotional sources, and dealt with the abstractions of peace and understanding that Ede could feel within his groups of stones, plates and glass almost as much as within his paintings by Alfred Wallis or sculpture by Gaudier-Brzeska.

My account is somewhere between the two – perhaps closer to Praz in spirit for the collection catches more than a little of the character of the collector. The start, logically

opposite: Detail of the eastern section of William Crawford's map of Dumfriesshire, 1806.

enough, is the door into the house that became so when a small, sentry like porch was added in the 1860s during the Johnstone years. It is little more than six feet square, just bigger but plainer than our Glasgow vestibule but with room in one corner for the usual collection of sticks and crooks. On the wall above them hangs the skull and horns of a small African animal, mounted on the traditional wooded shield, part of a job lot absentmindedly acquired by my father at some forgotten, country house sale. There is little space for anything more, apart from pairs of Wellingtons in a neat arrangement and in various colours.

Like many of its kind, Polmoodie has a little hall inside the door and a further, even smaller one, to the garden side of the house. As a simple front and back arrangement, they make a stark contrast with each other, one light and bright, opening on to the pink flagstones of the garden, the other a rather empty waiting space beyond the porch with a cloakroom for caps and raincoats. The only furniture is an elm chest – or a Scottish form of a blanket box, carved with the initials E B – and nearby a chair, also of elm, which came from one of the grander rooms of the Old College of Glasgow and has come down in the world. Above the chest, wider by a couple of feet, is a map of the county of Dumfries by the surveyor William Crawford, published in 1806, when it noted the parish of Moffat had a population of 1,619. It was composed of several large sheets, mounted on linen, which when seen together made a dramatic outline in black and white – a sort of whale of a county. Apparently, the survey and engraving cost the satisfied magistrates £970 in all. When I bought the map in 1975 from a print shop in Victoria Street, Edinburgh, I was offered by the enterprising dealer a companion one for Kirkcudbrightshire, the next door county, which I foolishly turned down.

Such a map was traditionally part of the fixtures of any hall, something to look at while kept waiting and a way too of breaking the conversational ice. But it added nothing to the comfort of the room and was too practical to be accounted charming in any way. When we came here, this hall space doubled as a rudimentary scullery to the adjoining kitchen but I doubt if such an arrangement had been part of the Johnstone scheme of things. The sinks and pipes disappeared and I increased the formality of the space by fixing on the wall a marble relief of a Roman provincial farmer, sickle and grapes in hand and dated 206/7 AD. To a visitor of a classical cast of mind – there were a few – he could be identified as a sort of homely, family god, one of the *lares* and *penates* of the Roman house. He stares somewhat blankly at visitors and has eyes only for the map across the room, perhaps eyeing critically the Roman roads and the forts along Hadrian's Wall that Crawford had plotted so carefully and accurately. The farmer's name was Titanius and he came from what is now Turkey. The inscription, crisply carved at the top of his image, tells that it had been set up as a stele by his family –'to my sweet father, as a memorial'.

The kitchen off the hall and looking south was a further part of the Johnstone expansion of the 1860s when the house was reorganised with a more obvious social structure in mind. As a kitchen it works well – if a little cramped – and we eat and work at a beech kitchen table, made locally in 2002, and set in front of the two windows with a comforting view through the trees and across the valley to the hills. The floor of this room and all the others in the back area of the house were laid with rough quarry tiles that gave it a pleasant, rather homespun air, particularly as they were arranged in less than straight lines on an uneven surface. The tiles have aged well and make a delicate balance between worn and distressed.

Dining rooms are by tradition the soul of the house and supposedly the home of family rituals from birthdays to Christmases. For the rest of the time, it has little part to play in an informal house and has a greater role as a passage way to the other downstairs rooms. It is one step down from the level of the hall and in the older part of the house. There are three doors – two original – and little of the physical character of Mario Praz's grand room that had no less than four doorways 'in heavy frames of sixteenth century design'. But unlike his rectangular dining table, mine is circular and small, on a single pedestal that suggests it was for breakfast rather than dinner and does not need any formal arrangement around it of chairs and armchairs. The table sits directly in front of the fire, the other essential element for such a room, which is lit only when the table is used and we gather in front for warmth, as much psychological as physical. The grate is a cast-iron gothic one of the early nineteenth century and was acquired by me from one of my less than honest scrap dealers in Edinburgh. It works well and does not seem to suggest some yawning, black mouth waiting to be fed constantly like its companions in the rest of the house. A large log basket is nearby, filled with sycamore wood sawn up after the winter storms have wreaked havoc with the older trees. It is one of three downstairs and was made by what is modishly termed an artisan from Wigton in Kirkcudbrightshire, a serious craftsman with a good eye, but who set standards and prices too high and found being a jobbing gardener paid better. They are all about three feet tall with handles at the top and hold logs enough for two, non-exuberant nights.

A further shorter and broader door that leads into the study is an old one composed of six fielded panels – the only one of this sort surviving downstairs. It passes through a stout internal wall about three feet thick that opened into what had been the bothy and dairy where a back stair had been tucked neatly into the old kitchen flue. I have installed bookshelves, from floor to door head in graduated fashion, along two of the walls, leaving a third free with a window, overlooking one side of the garden, as a sort of visual breathing space. The books are arranged in two sections, gardening and art, though this allows a certain amount of overlap and architecture has crept in as well. Needless to say, I have moved on from my earlier days in Glasgow when books were supposedly organised according to the colour of their dust jackets – or so the story went amongst my more critical colleagues. The fireplace is a small, cast-iron one of the later nineteenth century from the Schoolar trove, and over it a modest half length *Portrait of a Young Architect*,

Portrait of a Young Architect by Adelaide Lenoir, 1806, in the study

chalk holder in one hand, leaning against the large plan of some classical church. It was painted by one of the large band of liberated, female artists and exhibited in 1806 at the Paris salon, then the heart of the new revolutionary establishment. She was Adelaide Lenoir, married to the founder of the original museum of Monuments Francais, who moved in the circle of the great David who drew them both – the kind of provenance that Mario Praz loved. Hanging where it does, the portrait looks at a nearby group of architectural fragments, some from Dunmore, others English, and a fragile marble panel from John Carr's Workington Castle. I have arranged this odd mixture after the style of one of Piranesi's archaeological prints of the 1760's – balanced asymmetry – and set them out on an adjacent window shelf. From the corner of an amused eye and with a rather supercilious glance, the architect can just about see an earlier watercolour of a classical ruin by the other architect Robert Adam. It is Titanius and Hadrian's wall all over again.

The study, rather like the dining room, has something of the character of a through road. There are two openings on either side of the fireplace, apparently carved out of the original chimney space, into which has been squeezed the small wooden staircase to two bedrooms above. The effect has been to form one largish room with a different character at either end – one bookish, the other less so. The sitting room part is dominated by two pieces of furniture, a sofa with behind it and against the wall a sofa table, both of the early nineteenth century – the Gibson years. They look towards the dark grey, marble chimney piece of the same period, which was salvaged from the ruinous Dunmore Park, the huge and rambling Tudor Gothic house in Stirlingshire. But for all that, Dunmore had a largely classical interior that stretched to this austere chimney piece from the business room, which I acquired along with some plaster fragments. Unlike many of such marble orphans up and down the country, it came with its grate of cast-iron and brass inlay intact and this set the colour scheme, black and yellow, for much of the rest of the room. Matt black is also the colour of the frame of a portrait of Sir Henry Steuart, the father of landscape gardening in Scotland and author of the popular *The Planter's Guide*, of 1828, that hangs opposite. As such, he was rather close to my heart. The painting had been sold to America just before the First World War and came back fifty years later, though minus much of Sir Henry's legs and all of the brief landscape view. He was shown seated but disturbed in his reading, perhaps by his daughter of whom there is a larger, companion portrait in the Perth Museum. All of which gives the painting its sharp sense of time and place in the Praz style.

The sofa appeared as a modified wreck in a Glasgow saleroom in the 1980s but its sturdy frame of solid beech painted to look like rosewood, its brass feet, and ormolu rosettes had all survived the various cultural storms reasonably well. A possible date of the early 1820s suggested its manufacture by the prolific, Edinburgh firm of Trotter and sure enough its brother appeared in a booklet called *The Georgian Interior*, of 1978. Even with cushions it is a comfortable rather than relaxing seat and it has 'the air of refined solidity',

apparently sought by Trotter's patrons of whom Steuart may well have been one. I collected as companions to the sofa a broken set of chairs – only three – painted black with the original gold pen work decoration of a musical theme. It may have been intended for some music room and an attentive audience unconcerned about comfort and horsehair seats: it has more than a whiff of Kettle's Yard austerity. In contrast, a well stuffed, window seat on top of a warm, skirting radiator offers both a view and access to a small, yew-hedged garden with a baluster sundial in the centre. The tall window provides light and a comfortable enough spot to see the room objectively and critically, catch the route to the other end of the house 'as the hunter follows his game', as de Maistre described the travels in his room.

Going in the other direction, through the dining room and into the little garden hall, the path, as it were, finishes in front of another chimney piece. This belongs to the small sitting room – the original parlour of the house – a room probably refashioned during the Johnstone years. The hall beyond is an essay in Minimalism in miniature. It holds two pieces of architectural sculpture, one medieval Irish, part of a simple Gothic window, the other a large Greek stele, crowned with a vigorously carved anthemion in marble. I think they may remind the house of its roots in stone, and make a bond with those of the hills and dykes of the valley, present through the glass of the garden door. It is a feeling I can well understand. Still, I have never been tempted by the sort of historical romanticism that actually wishes to expose physically the history hidden behind the walls or under the floors for that matter. It was an approach fashionable in fifties and best seen in the work of the Italian

above left: Dark grey marble chimney piece from the Business Room at Dunmore Park.

above right: Sir Henry Steuart, after Raeburn, from *The Planters Guide.*

architect Carlo Scarpa. Strangely enough, the Schoolar builders had caught something of this and in the course of their renovations did discover the original doorway to the house, now in the pantry, and found also one of the old, square dormers in an upstairs bathroom. They were pleased with themselves and encouraged me to expose them in some way or another – an engaging idea that I resisted.

The hall opens into what we have always called the small sitting room, a friendly title though it is the same size as all the other downstairs rooms. It suggests, too, a casual comfort absent from its formal namesake at the other end of the diminutive enfilade where the spirit of Minimalism reigns formally. It has two windows, the larger looking over the tiny lawn that shows the first of the modest snowdrops and later the early daffodils, the lent lilies of our Border spring. There is the usual amount of furniture grouped around the fire as sofa and armchairs, made by the traditional firm of Whytock and Reid in Edinburgh, but they are small in scale and suitable more for dwarfs than giants, as the latter have found. The chimney piece is also of a similar scale – stone painted as deep porphyry and from the unpleasant man at Dunmore – and has on the lintel shelf a surprising group of antiquities largely bought over a period from the dealer in such things, Charles Ede. Beneath is a neat, little basket grate in cast-iron, supposedly from the Carron Works at Falkirk of the 1780s, designed to take small lumps of coal and burn brightly. The wall beside it carries a large painting – *Westerly RI* – by the American hard-edged painter Pierre Clerk, of 1971, which I acquired from the artist himself a few years ago. It is in black and

Pierre Clerk, *Westerly RI*, 1971.

white and such colours shape and dominate the room with the green of the chairs as a poor rival. As a colour, or so I was told, green is a bad one to be avoided in the country where there is grass all around – better outside than in, was the prescriptive message. This may well be true, but here the grass is more often as not covered in snow or dead under frost and green is spring.

On one side of the door into the small sitting room, there is the oval staircase that leads upstairs. I am always pleasantly surprised by its naïve sophistication that appears out of step with the simplicity and economy of the rest of the house. It may have come about when the estate joiners, employed on John Adam's Moffat House in 1762, worked here a little later and were keen to show what they had learnt. Possibly too, it was an attempt to raise the modest standards of farm architecture and as such can be seen in the plan and staircase for Kinninmouth, a farmhouse illustrated in the *General View of the Agriculture of Fife*, of 1800. The builders of both it and Polmoodie were interested in moving standards forward and turning frugality into both a virtue and architecture. The stair repeated the design of Moffat House on a simpler scale, with cheaper material but still keeping much of the detail; the profile of the banisters mimic the original accurately and form the same tight composition when looked at from below. They seem even better when compared with those found in the extended part of the landing – sturdier and less balanced – made nearly a century later. Like its source, the walls were curved but supported wooden rather than stone cantilevered treads that have survived well. A further

The landing with a homemade American flag of c.1907.

exercise in the unexpected is the American flag that hangs boldly over the balusters of the landing. It was largely homemade with the extra stars added as new states appeared and joined the Union: it has 46, which meant it was finished about 1907 but possibly started ten years earlier when Utah acceded. It came from the basement of a family house in Brooklyn, New York.

Usually the upstairs of houses are a bit of a disappointment – bedrooms rarely matched the pretensions of the rooms below and are smaller and lower and modest. In his account, de Maistre was of little help because his apartment in Turin was essentially a bed-sit with no upstairs of any sort. My rooms were simple spaces; less demanding in their contents for there had been originally only two separated by some sort of box-bed arrangement. Such rooms needed little more than a bed, chest of drawers and the few odd bits and pieces that furnish a conventional bedroom of the more Spartan sort. It was a style that seemed appropriate for my Barnardo's box – humble, functional and garret-like with dormer windows and sloping comb ceilings. Most of the other rooms too have basic cast-iron grates, probably of the 1860s, which together with the black painted floorboards – some the original wide ones – and shelves of children's books and toys suggest rooms tucked away and almost forgotten. What the children made of it all I never knew, perhaps they expected to discover the entry to Narnia behind some cupboard door. There is a domestic view from the windows, looking through the yew arch into the fruit garden with the three great beeches – speak no evil, hear no evil, do no evil – towering virtuously at the bottom. But for all that, it is the sound rather than the sight of the river at the bottom of the field that sets the tone for the rooms – the endless susurration of water, comforting and soothing in windless, summer evenings and encouraging sleep. But later in the year the sounds are different and during the long succeeding winter nights, disturbing and far from peaceful.

Of the five bedrooms, one looks straight west and bares the brunt of any prevailing wind with only a few protests but plenty of peevish murmurs. The rest face the garden and are more sheltered. It was here one stormy, November night, as I read in bed a memoir of the great garden of Inverewe in the northwest Highlands, the weather outside changed and became worse. As luck would have it, I had reached the chapter on the great Inverewe storm of 1953 when the garden was almost blown away and trees and plants savagely

View over the garden in a winter mist.

uprooted and scattered. As I read on, the house took up the theme of the book with increasing groaning and creaking, as the gale outside rose and struck the building forcefully and repeatedly. From what I could hear and feel, the fate of Inverewe was about to be repeated as the room shook and banged and the gutters outside overflowed, filled by rain and blocked by twigs. I read on, desperate to reach the end and know whether the house and owners had somehow survived such calamity. They had, but only just. Sleep was difficult and in the early morning when I went out anxiously expecting the worse I found nothing untoward – all more or less in order apart from the odd branch or two and a grey, swollen river. The house had played its little joke, a practical one, and suggested that it would not do to take its moods too seriously too often. It was a cautionary tale as well and since then I have studiously kept the room for guests.

This room is at one end of a short and narrow corridor that runs along almost half the length of the house, from the staircase landing to a bedroom at the other end. It has a sloping ceiling with even light and so is a safe place in which to hang and look comfortably at works on paper. The larger drawings on the wall are architectural ones with half way along a striking watercolour of a picturesque castle by Robert Adam, next to a small view – little more than a glimpse – of the sixteenth century Crichton Castle, by his brother-in-law John Clerk of Eldin – both men castle maniacs in the eighteenth century tradition. It is a pleasant place to linger horizontally on a wet day and has something of the casualness of a sympathetic junk shop to make me feel at home. At the furthest end of this corridor is our bedroom and here I have a small picture by another William Johnstone, an almost local artist, who worked for a period just over the hill at Potburn where it was painted. He came from near Selkirk, worked in London, and returned to the valley in the 1960s to become the last sheep farmer there before it was destroyed by forestry and abandoned. The abstract landscape is called *Border Red*, a less than imaginative title given to it by the auction house who sold the contents of Johnstone's studio in 1996. In fact, it differed little in the turmoil of composition and dark colours from other works he made in London around the same time. Its relationship to place was more in his mind where a feel for the Border shapes and moods was always present.

There is little more to be said: Polmoodie is a modest place to make a digressive journey of any sort last for long. De Maistre ended his fanciful tour by looking through the old letters that he kept in his bureau – 'a prominent object that the traveller's eyes light upon, taking the route I have indicated'. Apparently, it induced in him a kind of reverie that ended with his realisation that both confinement and tour were over and without so much as a backward glance he set off for the porticoes of the Strada della Po in Turin. But not of course for me: I belong to the Ede and Praz camp in which there is always room for something more, somewhere in the house and a sentimental journey to begin – 'Poor Animal! Take care' – de Maistre's closing warning.

OUTSIDE

One of the more perceptive warnings given to us by the Wilsons of Roundstonefoot was that for every hundred feet the land rose, you lost a day of light. They pointed out that Roundstonefoot was half way up the valley – that is with Craigieburn at the bottom and Birkhill at the top – so we should expect the growing season to be short, limited and deeply disappointing. Warming to his theme, Wilson maintained that the climate and gardens got visibly worse, house by house, as the road ascended the valley and climbed into the hills. Certainly, the small and somewhat ramshackle country house at Craigieburn seemed different, having a garden more decorative than useful and so outstandingly at odds with the frugality of the other farmhouses in the valley. At least, that was the gist of what the guide books of the nineteenth century claimed when they extolled its setting in a deeply wooded glen, rocked by the thunder of a burn that fell with tremendous force into the Moffat Water. It was here that some of the earliest dykes were built in 1783 and where the first of the ornamental conifers were planted and prospered – sufficiently so that by 1858 they formed 'colonnades of stately and venerable trees, such as have few equals in Scotland'. It was the home too of Jean Lorimer, of Robert Burns fame, who went to a party at Polmoodie in 1796 never to return home, eloping to Gretna Green: a sad tale and present in my mind as I pass the later lodge gates.

The road, the A708, has always followed an erratic path up the valley, connecting one farm with another, four on one side, three on the other. Nearly all of them had, at one time or another, gardens of a traditional sort, that is to say a rectangle beside the house, usually facing south and growing a few flowers and berries. Of them all, Roundstonefoot was the most sophisticated. The Wilson's predecessor had made a small water garden out of the burn beside the house and planted it in a rockery style, close to the bridge that carried the road past the house. The diminutive scale of the tiny plants beside the angle of the bridge reminded me of a Chinese garden shown on some blue and white Milton plate, as perhaps the Wilsons intended in some inscrutable way. Sheltered by a few largish trees, their range of alpine plants had prospered well enough as the more delicate ones were hidden by a high bank and protected from frost by the fast-moving water of the burn – a wonder to all. They had at the back of their minds an idea that I might attempt something similar, after all Polmoodie was in alpine country where the hills supported some rare Saxifrage and unusual ferns, all of which had excited both the local guidebooks

opposite: Remains of shelterbelt of Scots pine at Muchra.

and the National Trust when it arrived there in 1965. They were anxious that I should explore this sense of place.

The whole business had been set rolling with the original publication in 1857 of a *Narrative of a Ramble among the Wild Flowers of the Moffat Hills* and followed a year later by the *Guide to Moffat and its Walks and Wells*. Apparently, the rare fern – oblong woodsia – had been discovered at that time and was then virtually eradicated by the over-enthusiastic Alpine Clubs. It was rediscovered in 1954 by the botanist Derek Radcliffe and again in 1972. He had lodged with the Borthwicks at Polmoodie during the 1950s and wrote a feeling account in his Dumfries and Galloway volume of *The New Naturalist Library*. He was keen on the fern and even keener that it should remain in place, 'left to grace the bleak rocks where it belongs, as a reminder of the last Ice Age'. Such a mood was not uncommon and the frontispiece to *Moffat and its Walks and Wells* showed Dobb's Linn, almost opposite Birkhill, as a chasm where the mountainous rocks joined the clouds with a solitary tree hanging on near the top in a thoroughly romantic fashion. There is an equally solitary female figure shown taking a basket of food possibly to the fugitive Covenanters hiding in a cave half way up the cliff face and so giving drama and scale as well as history to the setting.

above left: D.O. Hill's view of Dobb's Linn from *Moffat and its Walks and Wells*, 1858.
above right: Photograph of Dobb's Linn in c.1905.
opposite: Looking up Dobb's Linn from beside the road.

The lonely tree on its rock, or some such sublime composition, symbolised this end of the valley before the onslaught of the conifer plantations. Apart from such isolated trees, there were small groups of birch on the higher and thinner soils and, on the sides of exposed cleuchs, outcrops of willow and alder, hidden from the scavenging sheep, and surviving through thick and thin. Such a natural-seeming landscape had been formed by grazing sheep and the need to control them by dykes and stells. A little later, rectangular, shelterbelts of Scots pine appeared and dotted the hillsides, rather like toy fortlets in some sheepish war. All was now in decline, the walls of the stells and shelterbelts ruined and the trees within dead or senile. To any traveller passing this way in the early fifties, it must have seemed like some subsistence landscape where farming had lost heart and little survived of the revolutionary drive of the later nineteenth century. Only the cars dotted around the basin of the Tail Burn pointed to the new development of the ten-minute tourist and the new kind of traveller. But come dusk at the end of a long afternoon or a winter's day, they were gone – until tomorrow or next year, only the litter marking their fleeting passage. Looking around, it was clear that the heart of such an enterprise lay in the farmhouse and steading, visible from both ends of the valley and encircled now by its few, huge sycamores. A closer view, showed the buildings in disrepair and falling into disuse with its guardians now the marauding sheep.

It was during some of my first journeys along this road, past the now familiar farms of

Photograph by Mrs Cameron c.1905 of Bowerhope garden from the Loch.

my neighbours that two things became clear in my mind: first that I should stick with the character of the garden in the same way as I did the house and, second, I should take my time – too much, too soon, was another Wilson piece of wisdom. Sad to say, the imaginary gardens of the manse or Barnardo's box were of little help. I was quite dismissive of them, certain in my imagination that they would be filled with roses and hollyhocks, bright and fussy, like the watercolours of Helen Allingham, but with little sense of place. Still, there were some of the more distant manses that had retained their glebe field, along with a scattering of large trees around the garden and they were close to the style of things I found at Polmoodie. Better still, I had come across some old photographs of the Bowerhope garden that gave a not unattractive sense of time past as well as suggesting what might have been planted here at some stage. I could easily persuade myself that such images were the spirit of the place. And, just as easily. I could see that the small abandoned garden with its crop of wild raspberries, exploding rhubarb, and fragmented walls was a document waiting to be read.

I don't think I ever took seriously the suggestion that the garden should imitate the bleak character of the valley and its plant life. It was the wiseacre Wilsons who suggested a rock garden in this spirit. They pointed out that a true alpine like rhubarb grew well enough here and that I had within earshot – more or less – the falling water of the Grey Mare's Tail and its glacial history of fossils and glyptolites, all of which should encourage a wilderness style. In fact, they were enthusiastic for me to explore some kind of Zen garden with a symbolic arrangement of the stones and rocks taken from the river and set between neatly raked paths. A little planting of a primitive Ginkgo or Glyptostrobus could be worked into the composition and their stunted forms would not seem out of place amongst vegetation regularly savaged by sheep and goats. However, a quick glance at the photographs of like gardens in China or Japan discouraged all such wild ideas.

About this time, I came across a copy of a small book with the title *The Valley of the Silent Loch*, which was published locally around 1920. The author's wife, Amy Cameron, had taken the thirteen photographs with which it was illustrated and this included one of Bowerhope and the garden. The house also had a certain literary distinction at the time, having been rented by the author Maurice Hewlett in the early 1900s. One of his short stories – *The Death of a Sheep* – made rather grim reading, its realism very different from the romanticism of Hogg's poetry about the same hills if not about the same sheep. Mrs Cameron's photograph was grey and grainy and showed the house from a compact garden, covered in creepers and with a tall yew to one side. The text described a sundial before the door with 'clipped yew and high box edging in the garden behind, sheltering tiny pale-hued cyclamen'. It claimed as well that the sun always shone here, though this was barely obvious from the photograph, and quoted that 'Heaven may be a bonnie bit, but gie me Bowerhope'. But it was the farmhouse style that appealed to me more than those of Roundstonefoot or Craigieburn, and I saw in the overgrown formality something of

Bowerhope from across St Mary's Loch, forestry felling underway

the old garden here, catching too the character of the house. But, like so much else, the Bowerhope garden has gone, the farm itself reduced to few fields beside the loch: the rest lost under a commercial forest of blanket-like proportions, ripe for felling.

How the large and small fitted together in the valley was always something of a mystery – a balancing act between hills, water, road and houses. There was too the logic of grass, sheep and shelter that formed a practical whole as well as making visual sense. All of this appeared to have been upset with the arrival of commercial forestry, its demanding road system and short-term employment that turned a sensitive balancing act into a brutal monopoly. Such farms as remained were reduced to a few hundred acres along the valley bottom and grazed by the more profitable cattle. But less hardy than sheep, they needed shelter and feeding – never cheap – and soon the farmyards acquired large open sheds out of scale and character and in the end barely profitable: livestock farming in the wrong place. It was a sad sight and an unnecessary one for I was quite sure that there was an alternative to the Commission's harsh measures that would allow sheep and trees to form an economic existence. A pattern of commercial planting could be devised that would follow the contours of the landscape, preserve the historic sheep runs, and balance sheep with trees along the hillsides and valley bottom. Instead, and almost perversely, the Commission followed and expanded the geometric style of the old shelterbelt. These isolated and angular squares and rectangles, thickly planted with Scots pines, had indiscriminately disfigured the hills and agitated Sir Walter Scott during his travels at the turn of the eighteenth century. There was little room for anything informal or casual-seeming in the Commission's scheme of things: to them sheep and shepherding were as much things of the past as the deciduous tree and the production of food was a thoroughly old fashioned idea.

What I had in mind was the mixture that I had come across when looking at Henry Moore's sculpture at Glenkiln. There, a grouse moor, trees and a public reservoir fitted neatly together and formed an effective middle and distant ground for the sculpture and furthermore accommodated the sheep – a Moore favourite – as a moving element in the huge landscape. In fact, it had been sufficiently inspiring to encourage me to try something similar but more modest when, around 1990, I approached the dealer of the Scottish sculptor William Turnbull for one of his Cycladic figures but developed

Henry Moore's *Standing Figure* of 1950 at Glenkiln.

cold feet about money and suitability. The valley was really too big and far too elemental for such things and a large sculpture would certainly strike a false sense of possessiveness – rather like planting the flag in Antarctica. In this I was right unfortunately, for a few years later one of the Moore figures was vandalised and the others prudently removed.

Forestry had been undertaken in several stages in the early seventies, guided as much by experience as public outcry. The areas that I now owned had been planted by Mr Gutch in 1977 and had involved the well known and tactful designer Sylvia Crowe, engaged as much to mollify local outrage as anything else. Apparently, it was she who suggested a staggered outline for the plantations, leaving clear the natural skyline of the hills. She also persuaded the Commission to put in some hardwoods – sycamore and beech – along the edges of the valley bottom but they were too few to have much effect and were easily overwhelmed by the more vigorous conifers. This forest was at its most unattractive on the steep slope above the river and facing the house, as luck would have it. The straight side of the rectangle was hard up against the Bodesbeck dyke, conscientiously rebuilt in 1923, with the top and its puny trees managing to obscure the skyline for most of the time. Luckily, the top plantations of Sitka spruce were more or less worthless and taking them down when they reached the desirable forty year mark would not be commercially viable. To fell them in a rough outline, well below the hilltops, and leave them to decay seemed the more sensible and pleasing alternative. Unfortunately, it would be an expensive one in man hours and requiring an inordinate amount of paperwork from the Commission in its Forest Authority role, now the self appointed guardian of our woods and forests. I had intended to open up as well a cleuch burn, buried in the plantation, so that it would split the wood vertically into two unequal parts in a natural seeming arrangement. This could make the scattering of sycamore at the bottom more visible and so link the forest to the tree groups of the fields along the river. I resisted the prescriptive attitude that demanded only native trees – really birch, alder and pine – and added beech and some of the silver firs to give different shapes and colours to the clumps. After all, my nineteenth century predecessors had been rather fond of the alien horse chestnut – introduced of course by the Romans.

It also became clear to me that the large blocks of conifer were not only out of place but out of scale and needed to be tamed or made human by plantations seemingly haphazard and domestic. I made a casual start in this direction in the early eighties with a new farm track leading from the main road and running down one side of the old shelterbelt to the river and bridge. It was intended for a tractor or pickup going to the three large fields on the other side of the river and was meant to be shaped by their weight and frequency of use: the old idea of function influencing form. On either side of the track I planted beech with behind it a scattering of oak and sycamore along the roadside that merged with a new shelterbelt of birch and pine that I had formed further along to the east. The overall effect was a foreground to the heavily planted hills when seen across the river. I continued in the same spirit on the other side of the house – that is to the west and the sheep grid. This was a much more ambitious undertaking. The plantation followed the curve of the Moffat Water and ran up to the roadside, where I again used beech with some pine, the latter to stand out in winter and give perspective of a sort. It made a long sweep down the hill towards the house and then opened to a short and fleeting view of one side of the building and the yard beyond. On the other side of the road, I had put in a few single sycamores for balance and found, quite fortuitously, that in springtime a wide stretch of bluebells appeared and flowered exuberantly before they disappeared under the density of thick bracken. The upshot of all this work was that the house and its setting made an inseparable part of the of the landscape that spread casually to the foot of the planted hills.

At the bottom of this track and just after it crossed the bridge, there was the rather raw banking to the river with its clutch of steel mesh inlets now more or less transformed into my river walk that led to the start of the second, conifer explosion. Just before reaching it, a water-gate spanned the river intended to keep the sheep out of the wood. I set in front of

Roadside beeches at Polmoodie planted in 1990

it about five large, flat topped, boulders from the hillside above that were to serve as stepping stones from one bank to the other in a rather casual way. It never worked particularly well and soon a spectacular flood moved them further down, set them deeper into the riverbed, and in an erratic fashion formed an effective waterfall – the river's answer to such foolish affectations. Beyond this water-gate, the river was left to itself and the shapes of the plantations along its banks were determined by wind and water and to some extent by Sylvia Crowe's porous wind breaks. The river continued eastwards to its source at the head of the valley and it was easy in the drier summer months to walk up the bed rather than the parallel road and feel what had been done so often in the past: it was the perfect memory map. The experience was similar, but less extreme, to that found by Richard Long in his *Coastal Walk across Scotland*: 'Walking in and out of Rain Squalls / Fording three rivers wading along flooded roads / Following a river flowing at three times walking speed / Walking towards a rainbow arching across the road ahead'.

Work in this respect was limited to my end of the valley and could not disguise the large, conifer plantations both before and after Polmoodie where forestry had pushed shepherding out and confined the sheep to the valley floor. Most of the hill tops were swathed in green and in some cases they formed a different skyline, broken by the gaps and rides between blocks of trees where the sky could be seen like a new range of hills. The old and comforting scattering of small squares and rectangles was lost, as were the burns and little valleys – the hopes – that divided up the hills from one another and changed character with the time of year. The removal of the sheep too had meant that without their close grazing the contours of the hills lost form and any sense of light and shade. It had been a gradual process of stops and starts as the economic fortunes of hill farms had worsened in the course of the last fifty years. Sheila Forman, in her record of the valley for the *Statistical Account* of 1958, described how much planting had been undertaken since 1947 and that was more than a decade before Derek Radcliffe's appearance at the door of Polmoodie, wheeling his bicycle. Little of this state of affairs appears to have disturbed the local author Molly Clavering, whose popular *Far From the Border Hills* described her brisk trip up the valley with her 'black dog' – not depression I think – in 1953. She noted that after passing Craigieburn, the Forestry Commission's plantations had already appeared on both sides of the road but beyond Roundstonefoot little had changed, ' the trees are left behind' as she and her dog made their way east. Her approach to the landscape was uncritical and descriptive, keener on the weather and the odd dose of local history, yet sufficiently observant however for her eye to catch at Polmoodie a 'little home-made notice on its fence announcing tersely in chalk 'Cigarettes sold here', a ruse by which the farmer could legally sell rather than give them to his addicted shepherds, as she failed to explain.

INSTEAD OF ARMS ON GOLDEN CREST
HIS HARP WITH MIMIC FLOWERS WAS DREST
AROUND IN GRACEFUL STREAMERS FELL
THE BRIAR ROSE AND THE HEATHER BELL.

VALLEY

Beyond Birkhill, over the pass and at the head of St Mary's Loch, there is a statue to James Hogg with The Ettrick Shepherd as its by-line. It was carved in 1860 by the Dumfries sculptor Andrew Currie who had made a successful career in recreating characters from the works of both Hogg and Walter Scott. Hogg was shown seated, larger than life, and in the familiar costume of his portraits with his dog Hector, a singing collie and his 'towzy, trusty friend', neatly carved at his feet. He faces westwards and looks over the loch to the distant hills where his shepherding days had begun and his pose and detachment have always put me in mind of Henry Moore's *King and Queen* at Glenkiln – not that Moore had seen either monument or Glenkiln for that matter. Hogg's working life had been spent in the area around the loch, as had his father's, and he had a deep sympathy with the people and an understanding of their traditions. His short novel, *The Brownie of Bodebeck*, was set largely in this eastern end of the valley that had changed remarkably little since the later seventeenth century. The farms remained the same, as did the family names of their tenants, and so did the harsh weather that shaped the strange story.

Unlike his rival Scott, for whom the valley was little more than a difficult route from east to west, Hogg wrote with feeling, greater imagination and a wayward sense of history. His story of *The Brownie* was typical enough. In this, a local and traditional tale, strong on people and place, history is turned into a battle between good and evil with a gripping dose of the supernatural. The Bodebeck of the title was the farm next door to Polmoodie, now known as Bodesbeck, where the possible Brownie cave remains, and where the events, correctly pin-pointed by Hogg to September, 1685 took place. It was at this time that a sharp and bloody campaign was conducted by the royalist Colonel Graham of Claverhouse to root out the fugitive Covenanters from the remoter hills around Birkhill to which they had escaped after defeat at the minor battle of Bothwell Bridge. Hogg had no liking for Claverhouse, the professional soldier, committed to the destruction of the Covenanters and intolerant of the local community's tradition for justice and generosity. In the tale, Claverhouse was contrasted with the equally independent, shepherd hero, Walter Linton of Chapelhope, and both were given the familiar Hogg brush with the supernatural – after all his grandfather had apparently seen and spoken to the fairies. Claverhouse was described 'as galloping over precipices, and cheering on his dragoons, that all the country people who beheld him believed him to be a devil, or at least

opposite: Andrew Currie's statue of James Hogg looking down on St Mary's Loch.

mounted on one. The marks of that infernal courser's feet as shewn to this day on a steep, nearly perpendicular, along which he is said to have ridden'. For his part, Linton was able to take the frightening antics of the Brownie fairy in his stride and cope just as easily with a haunted room in his own farmhouse at Chapelhope. Hogg admired the independence and determination of both shepherd and soldier that seemed to match 'by many degrees the wildest and most rugged, and inaccessible (landscape) in the south of Scotland'. He was at pains to make clear the isolation of the shepherding community beside the loch where 'we never hear ony o' the news, unless it be twice a-year frae the Moffat fairs', and so deepen the intensity of his drama.

In their opposite ways, both Hogg and Claverhouse saw the eastern end of the valley as a place of refuge and isolation. The farms from Capplegill to Chapelhope at either end provided various hidden valleys or hopes that were criss-crossed by the spread of the haggs – marshy hollows on the flat moors – where sheep and men could hide safely for long periods of supreme discomfort. Hogg moved his story from a historical drama in the style of Scott to something more exciting with the overlay of the legend of the Brownie, who was traditionally described as a 'benevolent household sprite, usually shaggy and of peculiar shape, who haunted houses, particularly farmhouses'. The same figure appeared in more alarming form in his *The Brownie of the Black Haggs*. Such wraiths and apparitions were all accepted unhesitatingly by the shepherds on a farm like Muchra, for whom they

Chapelhope of the Lintons from the road at St Mary's.

were part of the 'whole hordes of spirits that had taken possession of their remote and solitary dells, and of whom they lived in terror and consternation'. In this fashion, Hogg successfully raised the level of the action to one where there was a deeper, more elemental struggle between the forces of good and evil. He gave it, too, an almost heroic quality where the ruthless Claverhouse hunted men with the same determination as the shepherd guarded his sheep and over the same hills. He put to effective use his knowledge of place and events and described a society that had not greatly changed since his father and grandfather's herding days around St Mary's Loch. He knew all the farms at first hand so that his casual mention of names gave truth and accuracy to the events and surroundings. A fair instance was when Claverhouse took a prisoner to Dumfries, 'through the hills of Polmoody', the night was spent at Capplegill, where he had requisitioned the cow house in which to lock up his charge. It is still there.

For the want of much else, farmhouses were Hogg's essential landmarks that he used to pinpoint the events of his tale and give them an unmistakable sense of place. Apart from Linton's Chapelhope and its near neighbour Riskinhope, he mentioned the other remaining farms in a ten mile stretch – that is Polmoodie, Muchra, Capplegill, Bodesbeck. The names and the character of their tenants were of greater interest to him than the architecture of the farmhouse or anything of that kind. Chapelhope was the only building described in any detail as a 'new elegant farm-house', built close to the site of its predecessor of which a remnant survived adjoining the new house and was a key element in the novel as it unfolded. He dated the new work to the 1670s. It was at Chapelhope too that he allowed an occasional glimpse of benign weather beyond the thick mist and perpetual damp that shrouded the sheltered valleys. There, on a September morning, the ground near the loch was 'covered with a slight frost rime and a cloud of light haze slept upon the long valley of water', and with it, Hogg cautiously hinted at better things to come. But the more normal bad weather pointed to unhappier, even evil, events and for good measure he quoted the alarming Covenanting Midnight Hymn: 'Our morning dawn is with clouds o'erspread, / And our evening fall is bloody red; / And the groans are heard on the mountain swarth; / There is blood in heaven, and blood on earth'.

Most of the farmhouses mentioned by Hogg have remained as sheep farms though on a much reduced scale. He could easily find his way from one to the other, for superficially they look much as they did in his day. However, the hills where he shepherded are not the same: forestry has seen to that. A few cottages have appeared along the road – notably Birkhill – which are absent from Hogg's account of the late seventeenth century topography and probably appeared in the following century with the recasting of Polmoodie. Like the farmhouse, they have also moved on and are now slated rather than thatched and are cleaner, bigger, and dryer as well as painted a demanding white. All such changes were part of a much greater one that saw the horse and its stable replaced by tractor and garage, which in their turn have given way to the agrocat, the Land Rover, and the equipment for

View over hills towards Lock Skene and Tweedsmuir.

spraying and dosing. The circular stells and holding fields of intense shepherding have been abandoned, and the shepherds themselves become a dying breed along with the working collie. The walled lambing enclosures and those for dipping and branding are now redundant and the surrounding stone dykes largely in disrepair: the landscape itself has regained something of the open and wild character so feelingly described by Hogg before the agricultural revolution rolled up the valley.

A great deal of the character of the valley, evoked by the Brownie tale, was later captured by two of its stalwarts – the Boas at Birkhill and Tibbie (Isabella) Shields at her cottage on St Mary's Loch. Neither of the places appears in the story though they may have existed in some sort of humble form as glimpsed in Hogg's *Tales and Sketches*, of 1837. Both cottages were beside a road; Birkhill at the top of the pass and the end of the synonymous path, that of Tibbie Shields just off the hill road to Ettrick. Both had expanded their roles and had become by the 1830s miniature sporting lodgings before their literary associations were firmly established. Walter Boa came to Birkhill as the out-bye shepherd (distant) for Polmoodie in 1830 where he would have lodged probably with John Broadbent. It was the wife of the latter – Old Jenny – who gained for the cottage its sociable reputation at which the 'gudewife might sing', so much so that that it was marked as the Birkhill Inn in the *New Statistical Account* of 1845. The *Moffat Walks and Well* of the same time quoted strangely and anonymously, 'Cheese and bread are my door-cheeks, / And pancakes the riggin' o't'. The Boas were an old, shepherding family, friends of Hogg who accommodated him at Birkhill in the 1830s when he went fishing or shooting in the surrounding hills. It gained further distinction when the geologist Charles Lapworth lodged there between 1872 and 1877 and astonishingly found space in the cottage to store securely his geological specimens in five drawers. Both places were admired by their lodgers largely for the wild out of doors they offered so readily, especially when this could be found without the laborious and difficult journey to some isolated spot in the Highlands. It was only a few miles from either cottage to the foot of the Tail – the Gray-Meris Linne of the past – where the twice weekly coaches arrived from the two rival hotels of Moffat – the Annandale and Cranston's – each with their garrulous driver guide.

The accessibility of the inaccessible was quite apparent when the fisherman Charles McGilchrist published his book *Birkhill – A Reminiscence by a Liverpool Merchant*, illustrated with a handful of competent but conventional watercolours by Isaac Cooke in 1899. There were nine illustrations, five of which were for the area around Birkhill and one was of the cottage itself. It had replaced that of Claverhouse's day, probably during Gibson's tenancy in the early nineteenth century, and the foundations of the earlier building are above the house in what are now the sheep pens. In Cooke's watercolour, it was a traditional cottage, T-shaped, one storeyed with three bays facing the road, and an extension to the rear. It was compact, so much so that it is hard to see how the several guests were housed in any comfort or even privacy. When McGilchrist stayed there in the 1880s, he listed 'a doctor and his lady, the artist and his – six of us in all, beside the old herd and his guidwife, two grandchildren, the young herd, two extra hands to help with lambing', and even a few tramps in the byre for good measure. It seems that neither the number nor the character of such visitors was unusual and it stretched beyond the practical geologist Lapworth to John Blackie, professor of Greek at Edinburgh University. Blackie had been sufficiently taken by the style of life at Birkhill to present a copy of one his books to the house, suitably and helpfully inscribed in Greek. Such a group of bookish sportsmen was the alternative to the trippers who came to stare and who stayed for a couple of hours, taking in the Tail, the Loch, and perhaps the entertainment of the 'gudewife', before returning refreshed to Moffat. But all were gone by Autumn, and the valley empty except for the shepherds, their dogs, the sheep and perhaps the restless spirits of Claverhouse and the Covenanters in the chill wind.

Few traces remain of the Romans or their predecessors apart from mounds and terracing, and possibly a fort of some kind at the foot of the Tail. Later inhabitants have gone leaving few footsteps behind apart from those in the forlorn and abandoned graveyard above the loch at St Mary's, close to where Hogg's malevolent curate had a church of a sort. The tombstones there – such as can be read – are largely of the nineteenth century and mark the graves of the parishioners of the surrounding and other areas – collectively 'a peaceful, simple race', and one which Hogg saw as 'these old heroes of the hill'. However, the heroes for Polmoodie or Birkhill are not here or in any one spot but scattered between Yarrow, Eskdalemuir and Moffat itself, and they make clear that the shepherds moved on, away, or retired: shepherding dynasties like the Boas were the exception. The old tombstones, broken and bent, are more marker stones in the turf than anything else, maintained by the sheep who have moved in and ironically tend their former masters diligently, as shown in the view over the loch from Hogg's *Poetical Works*. The stones seem modest and practical and 'share something of every date, and style, and place, an ownerless owner'. They are only a mile or so from Hogg's grandiose monument and look towards him and the loch as though seeking his voice to tell the history of the valley in which they had all struggled. Here was the old heart of the place. So I think we live in the distance at Polmoodie, perhaps detached, more interested spectators than actors, looking eastwards, watching and waiting patiently.

Even from statue proportions, Hogg could not see clearly Birkhill or the Pass and only in his mind's eye spot the hunted Covenanters straggling over the hilltops from Bodesbeck to Chapelhope with Claverhouse at their heels. But he could see the old Birkhill Path that they had followed, as well as the newer road of 1793 that came to Chapelhope, though not its successor a short distance further down the hill – the new A708. All of them passed close to the cottage that must have suggested fancifully some modern Rome with its three, converging roads. The cottage door opens abruptly onto the newer roads with a view at once over the smaller hills of heather and grass, stacked one behind the other, each

of a different colour and shape. Behind the cottage, a small stone mound marks the site of its predecessor, visible no doubt in the past to any traveller struggling through the hills to a journey's end at St Mary's Loch. But looking in the other direction, west from the door, the eye follows the road spiralling downwards to the valley bottom and along the river to a distant halo of trees that encircle Polmoodie. Both river and this stretch of the road mark out what was a kingdom of sheep with Polmoodie as its old capital and the cottage at Birkhill as an outpost on the eastern frontier. In such an interpretation, the sheepish inhabitants have the place to themselves mostly and switch nationality from Blackface to Cheviot to deal with food and weather and the ground beneath their feet. Still staring from the Birkhill door but looking west along hills topped by the glacier and carved by erosion, the broken strata of rocks forms a gigantic measuring stick marking time as well as recording the graveyard of Lapworth's graptolite inhabitants. Just below the top of the pass – above the present road – lies the thick turf of its predecessor that took Walter Scott, limping behind his coach, downhill to the west in search of local colour, copy and the hospitality of his patrons at Drumlanrig Castle. Before this view fades, Bodesbeck can be glimpsed on a good day and the route seen that the Brownie and his refugees followed along the hilltops to safety amongst the sodden, peat haggs around Loch Skene.

Such hidden and misty valleys, shut well away from intrusive eyes, are described rather puzzlingly as hopes – 'a small enclosed valley, esp. the upland part of a mountain valley'. There are plenty of them amongst the hills and as farm names as well – Winterhope is opposite Birkhill. But the biggest and most notorious of them all was the Devil's Beef Tub or the Marquess' Cattle Stand, a deep and large gap cut out of the hills and high and north of Polmoodie. It appeared in Scott's *Redgauntlet* where it was described feelingly as 'A d-d deep, black, blackguard-looking abyss of a hole it is', and had acquired early its reputation as providing a hidden shelter for stolen cattle and sheep. They were discreetly held there until the hue and cry had died down and they could be shared among the infamous Reivers as the spoils of theft. There were plenty of others, though much smaller, hidden deep in the Border hills, where many of them served as hideouts when the need arose. It would be nice to think of all such things in the past tense, but foolish, as any shepherd would tell you quietly. For there is only a thin line between exchanging straying sheep that have crossed the marches and keeping the more desirable: the old wickedness is still practised though in a more modern form. The ancient, Border practise of 'hot-trod' (tracing stolen goods) is as difficult as ever. The forestry roads and tracks make it easy to transport sheep speedily from hill to sheep float and then to the wide world and markets, losing the simple identification of ear tags on the way. The key element in all such operations is stealth and an understanding of both the land and the ways of hefted sheep; sad to say the rustler – the unattractive modern Reiver – is often a local man and the tracks he follows part of the old Reivers Road. It is little more than a continuation of the old game of hunter and the hunted, and one that both Claverhouse and Hogg knew well.

opposite above: The ruined churchyard at St Mary's Loch, looking west.

opposite below: D.O. Hill's view from the churchyard at St Mary's, from Hogg's *Poetical Works*.

Having lived here for some time, it should not be difficult to explain what is the genius or spirit of the place. It is easily the landscape – a harsh one, often elemental or brutal and with little that is soft or pretty in any way. The immediate impression is of emptiness too, a valley of overpowering symmetry, at times even majestic in its simplicity, but always formidable and lonely. Self-sufficiency is the key to both landscape and inhabitants: the genius neither speaks nor listens but points a finger. In all of this the fickle element – the demon – is weather that sets the pace for what can be undertaken and done and appears at times almost to repeat in miniature the arrival and departure of the glacier. It is the character of struggle that touches everything here and challenges the growth of trees and sheep, the maintenance of fences and dykes and river banks, the profitability of farming. Much of this might of course be written of many remote, northern places but this one is outstanding in the compactness and surprise of the location, as if a handful of the Highlands had been picked up and flung south. And forty years on, the descent from the sheep grid to the house along the old Birkhill Path still provides a shock and that must surely be the real genius of the place – the shock of the past.

In writing in this manner, it is always easy to see oneself as the hero – saving and protecting – a reformer rather more than an intruder. The sheep are perhaps the proof of such arrogance. Perhaps I should have respected better the traditions of hill farming and tried to revive rather than preserve half-heartedly what remained. I was selective: too keen on appearance. I restored the dykes and the stells but not the shepherding ways that used them or indeed the sheep that needed them, though I still have a shepherd, but as a partner, with his cohort of aggressive dogs. I should have considered more seriously a return to the Blackies of the Irving era that were certainly smaller, leaner and more versatile than the hefted sheep of the farm – their descendants: a case might be made for breeding backwards. The height of the dykes was largely determined by their size, in the same way that the farmhouse door and ceiling heights were constructed for smaller people, rather like me, and the sheep themselves moved in hirsels rather different from those of their successors. But much of this would have been against the rules and regulations of subsidy farming, constantly changing, where numbers called the tune and where – at one point – a farmer was paid to have the sheep removed and – at another – to buy a sheep quota to keep them. It was only a few steps away from descending into a risible museum of farming life.

A similar argument for leaving alone could be applied to the tree planting of the valley, but this was firmly out of my hands with the die cast a good decade before we arrived. Though the crofting counties of northwest Scotland had their way of life and agriculture heavily subsidised out of guilt or romanticism, hill farming and its traditions were less fortunate at the hands of the Forestry Commission and its cousins Forest Enterprise and Forest Authority. The prescribed forestry solution was to fell and plant in a forty-year cycle and this had already begun both in the lower valley and beyond Birkhill. There was little I could do. It was like watching the unfolding of a green form of the vicious

opposite: Looking west to the two roads meeting at Birkhill.

Sutherland Clearances of the early nineteenth century with the people and the hills gone, physically and visually. I was left in my Indian-like Reservation of the past, isolated and dedicated to the Johnstone regime of the 1860s when the house was given a decorative setting of elm and beech with the odd shelterbelts of Scots pine on the bleaker and closer hills. I continued planting after this fashion with the same deciduous trees that repeated the circles and lines that Johnstone had set out in a modest and formal way. This may have paid more than lip-service to the past and enough to make sure farming continued on the hills and I could expect to be woken in the morning with the barking of dogs gathering the Blackie sheep and have the satisfaction of hearing and watching the casual enactment of an old ritual. I might recall as well Hogg's dictum that 'Without the shepherd's dog, the whole of the open mountainous land in Scotland would not be worth a sixpence'.

Looking around the house, I realise reluctantly that I may have been just as selective within as outside in my arbitrary judgments. Perhaps I should have been less dismissive and worked more sympathetically with what remained of the Johnstone era in the various rooms. But here I returned to all the prejudices of the Glasgow flat where the past hung too thickly for my liking, blocking both light and clarity. The brown varnish and dark wall-paper, the linoleum strips and the fancy cast-iron I found here, all seemed like a further challenge along the way to my Barnardo's box. And while the Johnstone 1860s suggested a pattern for the landscape, indoors it was the original Irving regime of a century earlier, or rather my interpretation of it, to which I returned most often. The wooden curved stair-case with the simple profile of its banisters was the key to the doors of the house in every sense. It had survived unscathed, no doubt as much through disinterest than any obvious sensitivity to the past, for I am sure that nostalgia was not much of a Gibson or Johnstone characteristic. By chance, when looking through Peter Thornton's pantoscoptic *Authentic Decor*, I found an illustration of a Field Marshal's study in Silesia of around 1820, with wide, wooden floorboards, plain walls with little on them, and practical, Biedermeier fur-niture, all clear and clean. It held out an encouraging if fanciful picture of what the rest of Polmoodie might have looked like if spruced up in this fashion and about this time. It was a challenge to which I rose only hesitantly and my little study when it came about was far too comfortable for my Silesian counterpart to feel at home or at ease.

In all of this, I often paid attention in a casual sort of way to the different periods that restoration revealed, some easier to understand than others. No doubt, I have been far from consistent and by not settling on any clear date or any particular period, I have ended up with a composition of disparities where neither house nor farm buildings fit chrono-logically, though they may do so visually. All too often I have set the clock back to different times – the Irving or the Johnstone years – the better to catch and hold my sense of the appropriate and practical. My work has not been in any way a historical restoration and I have been driven more by nostalgia for that perplexing house lost in my memory that needed to be rebuilt by time.

I have already confessed to my shortcomings as an improver in the eighteenth century sense of the word. I am almost persuaded that doing more would have been the riskier course to have followed, for it often seems that any sort of radical change has brought more than its share of hardship to the valley. The derelict buildings of High Farming are proof of that, as are the miles of dykes built during the enclosure mania of the late eighteenth century. The conifer plantations of the sixties and seventies can probably be added to such a list. But despite all such change, the valley and its inhabitants have made the best of it and learnt to swim with the various shifts in the economic tides. My arrival in 1973 certainly caught the end of one such cycle where school, public telephone, postman on his bike were all gone within the next few years. Of course, they were little more than fly-by-nights in the history of things, of little significance when compared with the old road and its smattering of humpbacked bridges or the wayward and restless river, linking past to present. In the fullness of things, it is they who have taught change as survival and the need to serve and understand new masters. Still, I am uncertain that the familiar sight and sound of the shepherd and his dogs gathering the Blackies on the hill that I first heard with Mr Learmonth forty years ago will last, or that making my way home will be the same. I keep my fingers crossed.

above: Collies Sam and Sweep from Birkhill on the quadbike.

THANKS

I am most grateful to Terence Leigh, my neighbour at the more biddable end of the Moffat valley. It was his film of 1998, *Men of the High Ground*, which led me to consider writing the tale of this smaller valley and the surrounding hills to the east. As I have already given an account of the tame end of things in *A Garden in the Hills*, I have made this is a story of the wilder, tougher country in the footsteps of Terence.

In all of this, the various workmen played their parts worthily from the small world of Moffat. Many have gone, as sadly have several of the firms they worked for or ran. Of them, Alexander Schoolar and Son was outstanding: followed by Joseph Hyslop and Co., Drummond and Murray, Matchett and Co., in the house and W.J.Murray on fences and gates. In the other world of book publication, I was encouraged at the outset by Robert Dalrymple who later designed this book with skill and imagination. It was he who suggested that Andrea Jones would make the ideal photographer for what I had in mind. And so it has proved. They were enthusiastically abetted by Gail Lynch and Emma O'Bryen at Pimpernel Press. I am grateful as well to Patrick Elliott of the Scottish Gallery of Modern Art who introduced me to the photographs of Audrey Walker. Behind all this, I have had the eagle eye of my daughter Liadhain scanning my pages and challenging my words – all for my own good I am assured, a view seconded of course by her mother.

I owe much to Ian Stephenson, my resilient tenant at Birkhill for over twenty years, who has with his collies skilfully continued the shepherding tradition of the Border hills. It has not been easy. And lastly there are the Learmonths – the house, children, sheep and garden minders: they have seen us through thick and thin as we slowly made our way home. I am deeply in their debt.

INDEX

Adam, John, 79
Adam, Robert, 108, 113
Agriculture, Department of, 72, 77
Ailsa Craig, 44
Allan, David, *Penny Wedding*, 23
Annan River, 57
Annandale Estate, 7, 74, 82, 83, 88
Annandale Hills, 21
Auchindrain Farming Museum, 28
Auldton Farm, 88
Avery, Miss, 10, 33, 44, 45, 61, 79
Bakewell, Robert, 83
Barnardo, Dr, 9, 10, 24, 27, 33, 42, 55,
  63, 73, 98, 100, 102, 112, 119
Barsetshire, 28, 44
Bauhaus, 25, 27
Betjeman, John, 27, 35
Birkhill Cottage, 44, 45, 54, 55, 82, 86,
  87, 116, 133
Birkhill Path, 13, 21, 53, 81, 133, 138
Black Esk Head Farm, 83
Blackie, John, 133
Blanket Sunday, 19
Blythe, Ronald, *Bottengoms*, 24
Boa, Walter, 132, 133
Bodesbeck Farm, 14, 24, 45, 57, 70,
  73, 74, 89, 127, 133, 135
Border Forest Trust, 15
Borthwick, Robert, 44, 45, 89, 116
Bothwell Bridge, 127
Bowerhope Farm, 70, 118, 119
Boyes, Geordie, 87
Broadfoot, John, 87
Brooke, Rupert, 27
Brooklyn, New York, 111, 112
Brown, Lancelot (Capability), 33
Buccleuch Estate, 82
Buchan, John, 28
Burns, Robert, 82, 115
Bute, Marquess of, 52
Campbelltown, 28
Cameron, Mrs Amy, 119

Cappercleuch Hall, 32
Capplegill Farm, 13, 14, 57, 79, 87, 88,
  128, 129
Carron Works, 110
Chapelhope Farm, 127, 128, 129, 133
Church of England, 27
Church of Scotland, 25, 27, 28, 39
Citroen Ami, 18
Claverhouse, John Graham of, 9, 19,
  127, 128, 129, 132, 133, 135
Clavering, Molly, *Far from the Border
  Hills*, 125
Clerk of Eldin, John, 113
Clerk, Pierre, 110, 111
Cooke, Isaac, 132
Covenanters, 19, 127, 133
Craigieburn House, 18, 74, 86, 115,
  119
Crawford Moor, 82
Crawford, William, 13, 102, 104
Crichton Castle, 113
Crofthead Farm, 14
Crowe, Sylvia, 123, 125
Currie, Andrew, 127
Dalbeattie, 91
Danbury Palace, 99
Devil's Beef Tub, 135
Dobb's Linn, 116
Dumfries County Council, 72
— Prison, 57
*Dumfriesshire, General View of the
  Agriculture in the County of*, 83
Dunmore Park, 96, 108, 109, 110
Eardley, Joan, 44
Ede, Jim, 10, 92, 93, 101, 103
Edinburgh, Scottish National Gallery
  of Modern Art, 59
— Sun Alliance Building, 96
— University, 100
Eskdalemuir, 14, 133
Ettrick, 23, 76, 86, 132
Farnborough, 27

Fine Art Commission, 58
Finlay, Ian Hamilton, 58, 59, 92
— *Archie, the Lyrical Lamplighter*, 38
— *Midsummer Weather*, 58
Fonthill, 91, 93
Forestry Authority, 15, 77, 123
— Commission, 7, 9, 14, 18, 28, 29,
  32, 44, 45, 47, 49, 54, 55, 72, 122
— Enterprise, 138
Forster E.M. *Howard's End*, 10, 33, 44
Frick Collection, New York, 100
Fulton, Hamish, 22
Gaudier-Brzeska, Henri, 103
Gibson, Thomas, 7, 61, 70, 82, 83, 86,
  89, 98, 108
Glasgow City, 9, 10, 35, 36, 43, 95, 96
— Doune Quadrant, 35, 36, 42, 43,
  44, 65, 104, 105, 139
— City of Glasgow Bank, 37, 87, 88
— Kelvin River, 35, 36, 42, 95
— Maryhill, 36, 38
— Old College, 98, 104
— Rottenrow, 37
— School of Art, 41
— University, 43
Glenkiln, 122, 127
Gracie, Tom, 87
Green Man Head, 97, 98
Gretna Green, 82, 115
Grey Mare's Tail, 18, 19, 21, 45, 53, 82,
  118, 119, 132
Grimm, Jacob and Wilhelm, *Fairy
  Tales*, 14
Guggenheim, Peggy, 100
Gutch, Jimmy, 48, 73, 77, 123
Hadrian's Wall, 104, 108
Hean, Bill, 63, 70
Hewlett, Maurice, *Death of a Sheep*,
  119
Hill, D.O., 19, 135
Hirta, 53

Hogg, James (Ettrick Shepherd), 9, 23, 83, 128, 139
— *Poetical Works*, 133
— *The Brownie of the Black Haggs*, 128
— *The Brownie of Bodebeck*, 19, 74, 127
— *The Shepherd's Calendar*, 23
Hopetoun, Earl of, 23, 24
Hunterheck Farm, 9, 87
ICI (Imperial Chemicals Industry), 72
Inverewe Garden, 112, 113
Irving, David, 7, 23, 52, 82, 83, 89, 139
Jencks, Charles, 59
Johnstone, James, 87
Johnstone, Robert, 7, 61, 79, 82, 88, 89, 104, 139
Johnstone, William, 113
Kettle's Yard, Cambridge, 10, 11, 92, 98, 103
Kinninmouth Farm, 111
Laidlaw, Robin, 82, 86
Lane Fox, Robin, *Better Gardening*, 72
Lapworth, Charles, 132, 135
Learmonth, Elsie, 45, 61, 66, 74, 79
Learmonth, Peter, 73, 74, 140
Lenoir, Adelaide, 105, 108
Liebeneski, 94
Linton, Tam, 82
Linton, Walter, 127, 128
Loch Skene, 19, 135
London, British Museum, 93
— Sir John Soane's Museum, 93, 99
— Wallace Collection, 99
— Whitechapel Gallery, 53
Long, Richard, 21, 53
— *Coastal Walk*, 125
— *Touchstones*, 21
Lorimer, Jean, 82, 115
Louisiana Museum, Denmark, 98
Luxembourg Palace, 101
MacCaig, Norman, *A Man in Assynt*, 11
Mackintosh, C.R., 39
Macknaw Farm, 83
Maistre, Xavier de, *A Journey Round my Room*, 103, 109, 113
McCairns, Helen, 41
McGilchrist, Charles, *Birkhill A Reminiscence*, 19, 132
Marzaroli, Oscar, 36, 38
McIlvanney, William, 44
Manafon, 27, 28
Mazarin, Cardinal, 101

Menzies, Jack, 41, 42
Moffat, 11, 18, 74, 89, 104
— Annandale Hotel, 19, 132
— Cranston's Hotel, 19, 132
— House, 7, 79, 111
— Water, 9, 11, 48, 56, 57, 115, 124
Moore, Henry, 122, 123, 127
Morgan, Edwin, *Glasgow Sonnets*, 36
Mountbenger Farm, 86
Muchra Farm, 115, 128, 129
National Trust for Scotland, 7, 15, 40, 41, 45, 94, 116
Nicholson, Ben, 93
Nissen hut, 29, 32, 45, 63, 80
Perth, 28
Piranesi, Giovanni Battista, 108
Polmoodie, 7, 9, 11, 14, 18, 21, 23, 24, 37, 44, 48, 61, 63, 72, 73, 82, 88, 98, 100, 104, 113, 115, 125, 135
Portrack House, 59
Phillips Collection, Washington, 98
Potburn Farm, 113
Praz, Mario, 101, 103, 105, 108
— *The House of Life*, 93, 98, 101
Radcliffe, Derek, 61, 89, 116, 125
— *New Naturalist Library*, 61, 116
Rainsford Hannay, Frederick, *Dry Stone Walling*, 66
Read, Herbert, *The Meaning of Art*, 100
— *Innocent Eye*, 100
Rogerson, Geordie, 66, 67, 70, 74, 87
Rollin, Charles, *Ancient History*, 92
Roundstonefoot Farm, 14, 18, 24, 72, 73, 74, 86, 115, 119
— Hall, 29, 32
— Schoolhouse, 48
Royal Exchange, London, 63
Sailfoot Farm, 18, 74
Sartorius, John Nost, 94
Schoolar, John, 63, 64, 65
Scott, Sir Giles Gilbert, 43
Scott, Sir Walter, 81, 99, 100, 122, 127, 128, 135
— *Redgauntlet*, 135
Scott, William, 87
Selkirk, 18, 113
SEPA, 57
Sheep, Blackface (Blackies), 7, 15, 52, 53, 54, 83
— Cheviot, 15, 52, 83, 86
— Leicester, 83, 86
— Soay, 47, 52

Shields, Tibbie, 132
Sinclair, Sir John, 83
Silverstein, Shel, *Keep-Out House*, 81, 82
Southerness-on-Solway, Lighthouse, 25
— Smookey, 24, 25
St Just, Louis-Antoine de, 58
St Kilda, 52, 53
St Mary's Loch, 15, 70, 129, 132, 133, 135
Statistical Account, 23, 52, 83
— *New*, 19, 87, 132
Stephen, Henry, *Book of the Farm*, 87
Steuart, Sir Henry, *The Planter's Guide*, 108, 109
Stevenson, Robert Louis, 38
Stonypath (Little Sparta), 58, 59
Strawberry Hill, 91, 99
Sutherland Clearances, 139
Tait, Alan, *A Garden in the Hills*, 9
Taylor, Martin, 64, 66
Tennoch, William, 7, 83
Thomas, Edward, 49
Thomas, R.S., 27
Thomson, Alexander (Greek), 37
Thornton, Peter, *Authentic Decor*, 140
Threave Castle gardens, 63
Titanius, 104, 108
Trollope, Anthony, 28
Trotter, William, 108, 109
Turnbull, William, 122
Turin, Strada del Po, 113
Venturi, Robert, 63
Walker, Audrey, 37, 38
Walker, Robert, 87
Wallis, Alfred, 103
Walpole, Horace, 91, 99, 100
Waterfield, Hermoine, *Provenance*, 96
Waterhead Farm, 83
Waterhouse, Alfred, 93, 94
Wells, H.G., *War of the Worlds*, 54
Whytock and Reid, 110
Wilkie, David, *The Cottar's Saturday Night*, 23
Wilkins, William, 96
Wilson, Dr, 72, 115, 119
Wilson, Jimmy, 64, 77, 81
Workington Castle, 108
Yarrow, 86, 133

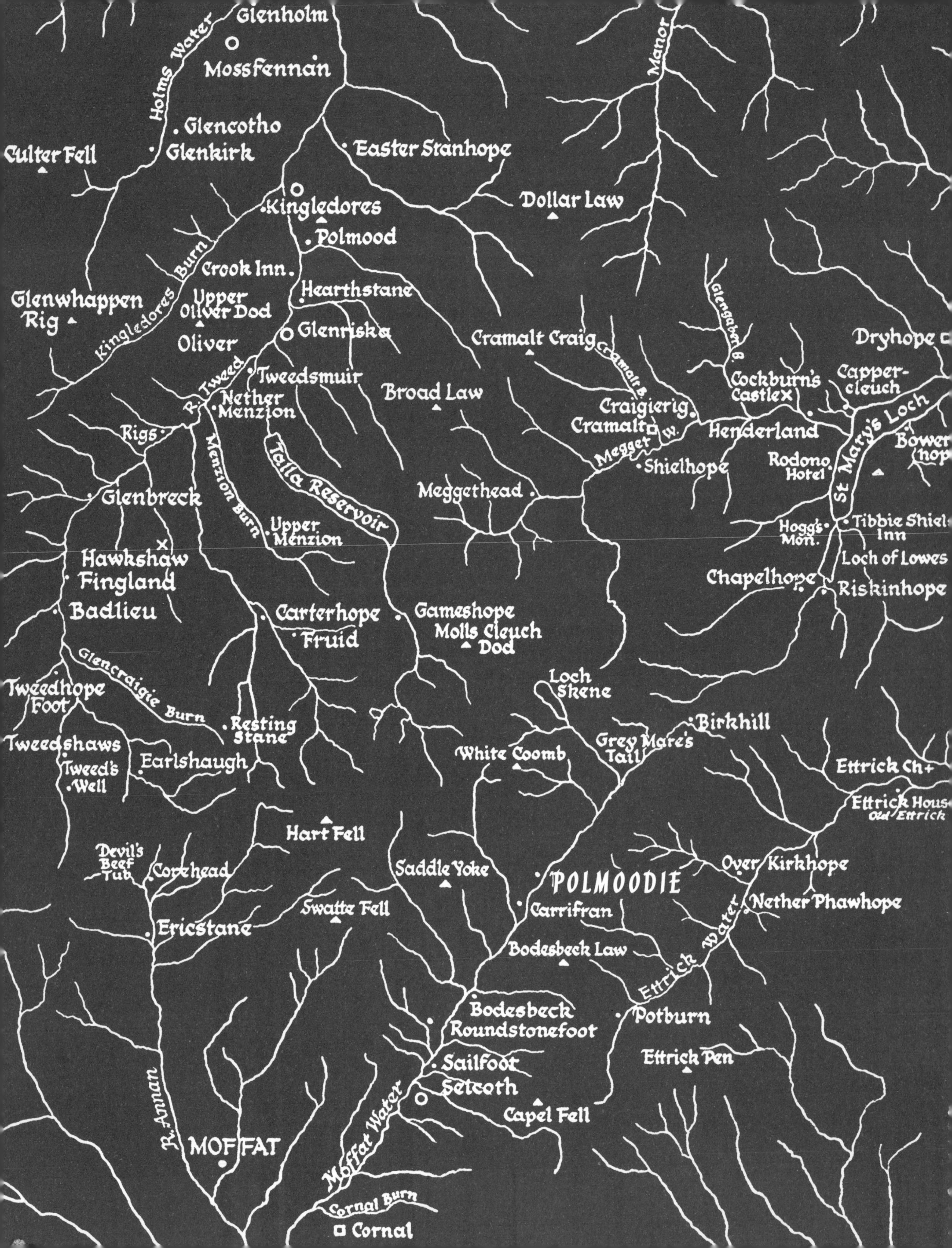
Glenholm
Holms Water
Mossfennan
Manor
Glencotho
Culter Fell
Glenkirk
Easter Stanhope
Kingledores
Dollar Law
Polmood
Crook Inn.
Kingledores Burn
Hearthstane
Glenwhappen Rig
Upper Oliver Dod
Glenriska
Oliver
Cramalt Craig
Cramalt B.
Glengaber B.
Dryhope
R. Tweed
Tweedsmuir
Broad Law
Cockburn's Castle
Capper-cleuch
Nether Menzion
Craigierig
Cramalt
Megget W.
Henderland
St Mary's Loch
Rigs
Bower
hop
Talla Reservoir
Menzion Burn
Shielhope
Rodono Hotel
Meggethead
Glenbreck
Upper Menzion
Hogg's Mon.
Tibbie Shiel Inn
Hawkshaw
Loch of Lowes
Fingland
Chapelhope
Riskinhope
Badlieu
Carterhope
Gameshope
Fruid
Molls Cleuch Dod
Glencraigie Burn
Loch Skene
Tweedhope Foot
Resting Stane
Birkhill
Tweedshaws
Grey Mare's Tail
Earlshaugh
White Coomb
Tweed's Well
Ettrick Ch+
Ettrick Hous
Old Ettrick
Hart Fell
Devil's Beef Tub
Corehead
Saddle Yoke
Over Kirkhope
POLMOODIE
Nether Phawhope
Swatte Fell
Carrifran
Ericstane
Bodesbeck Law
Ettrick Water
Bodesbeck
Potburn
Roundstonefoot
Ettrick Pen
Sailfoot
Setcoth
Capel Fell
R. Annan
MOFFAT
Moffat Water
Cornal Burn
Cornal